Music Library Association Technical Reports Series

Edited by H. Stephen Wright

D1261753

18. *Careers in Music Librarianship: Perspectives from the Field* compiled by Carol Tatian, 1990.
19. *In Celebration of Revised 780: Music in the Dewey Decimal Classification, Edition 20* compiled by Richard B. Wursten, 1990.
20. *Space Utilization in Music Libraries* compiled by James P. Cassaro, 1992.
21. *Archival Information Processing for Sound Recordings: The Design of a Database for the Rodgers and Hammerstein Archives of Recorded Sound* by David Thomas, 1992.
22. *Collection Assessment in Music Libraries* edited by Jane Gottlieb, 1994.
23. *Knowing the Score: Preserving Collections of Music* compiled by Mark Roosa and Jane Gottlieb, 1994.
24. *World Music in Music Libraries* edited by Carl Rahkonen, 1994.
25. *Cataloging Musical Moving Image Material: A Guide to the Bibliographic Control of Videorecordings and Films of Musical Performances and Other Music-Related Moving Image Material: With Examples in MARC Format* edited by Lowell Ashley, 1996.
26. *Guide to Writing Collection Development Policies for Music*, by Amanda Maple and Jean Morrow, 2001.
27. *Music Librarianship at the Turn of the Century* edited by Richard Griscom, assistant editor Amanda Maple, 2000.
28. *Cataloging Sheet Music: Guidelines for Use with AACR2 and the MARC format* compiled and edited by Lois Schultz and Sarah Shaw, 2003.
29. *Careers in Music Librarianship II: Traditions and Transitions* edited by Paula Elliot, associate editor Linda Blair, 2004.

Careers in Music Librarianship II

Traditions and Transitions

Edited by
Paula Elliot
Linda Blair

*Music Library Association
Technical Reports, No. 29*

The Scarecrow Press, Inc.
Lanham, Maryland • Toronto • Oxford
and
Music Library Association
2004

SCARECROW PRESS, INC.

Published in the United States of America
by Scarecrow Press, Inc.
A wholly owned subsidiary of
The Rowman & Littlefield Publishing Group, Inc.
4501 Forbes Boulevard, Suite 200, Lanham, Maryland 20706
www.scarecrowpress.com

PO Box 317
Oxford
OX2 9RU, UK

British Library Cataloguing in Publication Information Available

Library of Congress Cataloging-in-Publication Data

Careers in music librarianship II : traditions and transitions / edited
by Paula Elliot, Linda Blair.
 p. cm. — (Music Library Association technical reports ; no. 29)
 Includes bibliographical references and index.
 ISBN 0-8108-5004-4 (paperback : alk. paper)
 1. Music librarianship—Vocational guidance—United States. 2. Music
librarians—United States. I. Title: Careers in music librarianship
two. II. Elliot, Paula. III. Blair, Linda, 1955– IV. Music Library
Association technical reports (Lanham, Md.) ; no. 29.
ML111 .C33 2004
026'.78'023—dc22

 2003023981

For Suki Sommer

Contents

Foreword

Why a new *Careers in Music Librarianship*? The primary motivations for the 1990 publication by that name hold true for this new work: to examine perceived changes in the profession and to provide a current snapshot of the profession by describing "the challenges and rewards of a career in Music Librarianship."[1] Similarly, there have been changes in the profession and a desire to look at those changes more closely. There is a need "to address our practice after more than a decade of dynamic transition, describing our vastly different information environment, and discussing the wide variety of jobs now enjoyed by our colleagues."[2]

As before, the benefits of such an examination are meant for both those already inside the profession of music librarianship and for those outside. For those inside, a new *Careers in Music Librarianship* provides the opportunity to look at the larger picture—to examine the overall health of music librarianship and to consider what actions might contribute to its continued good health. For those outside the profession, it will provide current information as to what a career in music librarianship actually entails and attract newcomers to that profession. For once again, this book focuses on the practitioners of music librarianship.

Many articles have appeared describing the *collections* held by various music libraries. The *work* accomplished with these collections—cataloging, reference, preservation, and more—has also been thoughtfully described, notably by *Music Librarianship at the Turn of the Century.*[3]

Yet nothing in recent times has put these together and considered the *people* who are responsible for the collections and for working with them. What, besides a deep attraction to music, do music librarians have in common? What training do they have? Is there a typical career path, and what is found to be satisfying or frustrating about this path? How do music librarians keep up with changes in the profession and in their particular positions? Who will make up the next generation of music librarians, and what further changes might they encounter in their own careers? These are the types of questions and issues that this new edition wishes to address.

To accomplish this, the following essays look at each stage of a career in music librarianship: preparation and training, the job search, the possible job environments, career development, and professional development. The careers of future practitioners and what they may encounter are also explored. Finally, there is an eloquent summation of the fundamental values shared by all music librarians. All of the essays have been written by practicing music librarians, who share their expertise and experience.

While the description of music librarians' fundamental values concludes this report, it may be helpful to those outside the profession to read Sommer's historic essay first. Many of the other essays necessarily focus on differences within music librarianship. Yet there is a shared foundation, whether it is explicitly discussed or not. Music librarians make up only about .6 percent of librarians as a whole.[4] Those thinking of entering this tiny specialization would do well to realize that what sets us apart and makes our profession distinctive also serves to unify us.

Why a new *Careers in Music Librarianship*? In short, because many have found careers as music librarians to be rewarding and satisfying. This self-examination reveals the many shapes those careers may take, describes where they may lead, and outlines how one prepares for them. It serves as both an assessment and celebration for those inside the profession. For those outside the profession, it should prove informative and, perhaps, enticing.

On behalf of the Music Library Association's Personnel Subcommittee, I am pleased to present this report to MLA members and potential members. Many thanks are due to all the contributors, for their hard work and thoughtful analyses. Particular thanks go to the Editor, Paula Elliot, and Associate Editor, Linda Blair for their vision, determination, guidance, and tactful reminders, that brought this new *Careers in Music Librarianship* to light.

Jeanette L. Casey, Chair
Personnel Subcommittee of the Administration Committee
Music Library Association

Notes

1. *Careers in Music Librarianship: Perspectives from the Field*, MLA Technical Reports, 18, comp. Carol Tatian (Canton, MA: Music Library Association, 1990).

2. Paula Elliot and Linda Blair, proposal for the present volume.

3. *Music Librarianship at the Turn of the Century*, ed. Richard Griscom (Lanham, MD: Scarecrow Press, 2000).

4. This rough estimate was arrived at by comparing the number of personal MLA members listed in the MLA 2003 *Membership Handbook* with the total number of librarians estimated by the American Library Association. "America's Libraries: Some Basic Facts and Figures." (American Library Association, 2001), http://cs.ala.org/@yourlibrary/factsheet1.cfm_ (19 May 2003).

Preface

This book was planned as a report on the state of the profession of music librarianship, a study of the possibility for employment in the field, and a prognosis for its survival. What resulted instead is something both more personal and perhaps more useful: it is a set of reflections, opinions, meditations, and advice offered by respected professionals who reveal themselves to be deeply caring people, passionate about their profession—perhaps to a fault—who would all admit that they have fun doing their work. So you will not find any charts or graphs, though there is some analysis, and there are some numbers. You will not find a collection of objective studies, nor will you find a calculated recruitment or retention tool, though I believe that some readers will be attracted to music librarianship or find affirmation in a choice made long ago.

Sometimes, I have imagined that this book's obsolescence might precede its publication. In the year during which this book was put together, extreme budget cuts, downsizings, and reorganizations have become soberingly commonplace in our libraries. Notable exceptions aside, we currently live and work in a library environment where specialization is under threat, and the well-trained generalist appears to be the librarian most likely to survive. In this uncertain climate, it would be easy enough to despair for the future of music librarianship, but I would ask readers to wait a while for that. Our world is full of surprises.

Here, regardless of content, each chapter communicates an optimism that seems to surpass my gentle editorial admonition to "keep it upbeat." As I received each author's contribution, it became apparent that they fell together rather like a spontaneous conversation. Readers will see that some ideas expressed by one author are reinforced by another. Sometimes the authors disagree, and there are noticeable contradictions. Rather than impose consistency, I decided to allow each author an independent voice. Compiling this book has reminded me that the authors here represent a community, and that community represents something much more enduring than itself.

The chapters of this book are arranged as if to answer a series of practical questions: What do music librarians do? How do I get to be one? What happens after I've been one for a while? What's it going to be like down the road? Where can I look for support and professional development? What can I read to find out more? The last section, "About the Contributors," offers a rich response to the crucial question, "Who becomes a music librarian?"

If this book offers readers an honest view of the job options available to a certain group of people, if it offers one person a possible career option, if it offers encouragement to one music librarian who has indulged in despair, it fulfills its mission. And if history shows that it paints a rosy picture of a quaint and diminishing population, it speaks of the population that "cares for a manuscript by J. S. Bach and gets the newest CD for someone to take home and listen to." That is the way Suki Sommer, to whom this volume is dedicated, has described the work of music librarians. Despite economic vagaries and administrative fashions, there's a job to do. This book is about the doing.

The voices and the spirits of many people are on these pages. Without their presence, this book would be something very different. My associate editor, Linda Blair, thanks Daniel Zager, librarian of the Sibley Music Library of the Eastman School of Music, for supporting and encouraging her work on this project. She also thanks her colleagues Ralph Papakhian, Linda Solow Blotner, Geraldine Laudati, and Jennifer Bowen, for the material included in her chapter. She would like to acknowledge her husband, Allen, and her daughters Kate and Beth, for their moral support.

For their contributed chapters, friendship, advice, and encouragement, my thanks go first to Linda herself, whose work as associate editor and willing indexer is also gratefully acknowledged; and to Jeanette Casey, Laura Dankner, Renee McBride, Jean Morrow, Ned Quist, Sheri Stormes, Suki Sommer, Gordon Theil, John Wagstaff, Laurel

Whisler, and Steve Wright, who is also editor of MLA Technical Reports, the series of publications that includes this book. I am also indebted to members of MLA's Personnel Subcommittee who sat around a conference table early in 2002 discussing the idea of a new *Careers in Music Librarianship*. For my own chapter, many individuals responded to my requests for some conversation about their jobs and their careers. Their personal remarks, anecdotes, advice, and testimonials did more than provide quotations. They set the tone for the whole project, as they unexpectedly created for me a luminous and human picture of our profession. For their generosity, my deep appreciation goes to Alice Abraham, Kathy Abromeit, Leslie Bennett, Beth Christensen, Joyce Clinkscales, Jane Cross, Cathy Dixon, Mary DuMont, Margaret Erickson, Bob Follett, Susan Golden, Jane Gottlieb, Jon Haupt, Mickey Koth, Steve Landstreet, Richard LeSueur, Mark McKnight, Tina Murdock, Hollis Near, Vincent Pelote, Laura Probst, Cindy Richardson, and Anna Seaberg. Anyone inadvertently unrecognized has my sincere apology.

My thanks go to the Music Library Association for making this work possible; Virginia Steel, director of libraries at Washington State University, who approved the proposal that allowed for a year's sabbatical leave from my regular duties; and Karen Weathermon for her friendly editorial comments. Late-breaking appreciation goes to Nicole Carty, production editor at Scarecrow Press, for her attentive guidance. And heartfelt gratitude goes to my husband, Paul Brians, for his patience, generosity and companionship throughout this extraordinary year.

Paula Elliot
Fall 2003

1

A View of the Field:
Landscapes and Faces

Paula Elliot

If you accept the thesis that creative art is a species of communication, I would urge that the music librarian plays a vital part in this communication. I would go further and say that the very nature of music makes [the music librarian's] service quite distinct from almost every other branch of librarianship.

—Alexander Hyatt King[1]

The love of music and the ethic of service are elements that bind music librarians to the materials of their specialization, to their library users, and to each other. In choosing their profession, those who work with music in libraries have found a way to simultaneously support and engage in the field they care most about, while they share their enthusiasm for it and provide others with the means toward study and enjoyment.

The last decade of the twentieth century witnessed remarkable changes in the production and consumption of music. It also saw significant changes in research tools and methodologies and in pedagogical approaches to the discipline. And the increasingly pervasive accessibility of recorded sound had a profound impact on the world of libraries. In addition to the traditional physical materials of librarianship—books, journals, scores, reference publications, and sound recordings in various formats—music librarians are by now thoroughly acquainted with what might best be called "transitional" or "emerging" modalities for the delivery of information. A dazzling array of electronic resources supports all aspects of our work, standing alongside of the world's venerable treasury of rare material—ancient books and not so ancient, unique manuscripts, and valuable ephemera. It gives a librarian pause to consider that today's cutting-edge collections will be tomorrow's rare ones. The materials supporting the study and enjoyment of music have not so much changed as expanded, making new demands on our libraries and the people who devote their careers to them.

The 1990 edition of *Careers in Music Libarianship* defines several subdisciplines within the field of music: music history, ethnomusicology, theory, composition, performance, music education, and music therapy.[2] Since the appearance of that publication, our millennial culture has blurred distinctions between the traditional areas of musical inquiry and added new subdisciplines, such as the music industry and music information retrieval. Ethnomusicology informs traditional European models of music history and cultural studies. The world of mass entertainment affects critical taste and aesthetic preference. Experimental psychology, engineering, and computer science influence composition and theory. Music business and media production drive technological innovation, and technological innovation supports research. The reviewer Ivan Hewett has suggested that "a pop song can legitimately receive as much earnest attention as a Schumann song."[3] Perhaps *Musikwissenschaft,* the nineteenth century's term implying an all-encompassing knowledge of the field, has found its real definition and its practical application in today's interdisciplinary approaches.

And interdisciplinarity is utterly at home in a library.

Our music libraries offer resources for entertainment and self-education, as well as for scholarship and research. Whether in academic or lay conditions, inquiry into musical subjects often breaches the boundaries between separate disciplines. Along with performers and scholars of music, students in today's schools and universities visit their libraries to investigate music topics for class assignments in English, communication, history, political science, and anthropology, not to mention business and computer science. In our communities, working adults borrow sound recordings and videotapes from their libraries as often as they do books for recreational purposes.

While the specialized "music library" is the implicit home of the specialist "music librarian," it is limiting to restrict this discussion to self-contained music libraries alone. This discussion is more appropriately about *music in libraries*, and, more specifically, the *people* who care for music, select music materials, and provide music services, regardless of job description or institutional title. Some music librarians specialize exclusively in music, and others fold their specialization into a package of numerous subject responsibilities. To be as inclusive as possible, in this discussion a music librarian is a librarian who deals with music.

Our Users, Ourselves

Deborah Campana has observed that "the close association among music librarians seems to have evolved because of the mission we share—to collect, preserve, and make accessible materials and information on the subject to which we all are drawn."[4] This "subject to which we are all drawn" binds us not only to one another in professional practice but to our users in a common recognition of music's inestimable appeal. Bound by music, it is uniquely possible for us to see ourselves in our users, giving us a particular empathy with their needs. In providing people with the materials of music, we offer them something that is both immediate and immeasurable. Every aspect of our work allows us to support human imagination and celebrate creativity, past and present. "What is it that releases all the energy and the power we have gathered and made available?" asks Michael Gorman, the eminent librarian-thinker. "The presence of the people on whose behalf we work."[5]

Who are those individuals for whom we do our work, those library users who justify our varied careers? They are musicians, professional and amateur. They are music lovers, some possessing a high degree of sophistication, others who simply "know what they like." They are academics and scholars: musicologists, historians, theorists, ethnomusicologists, and a population of music statisticians and computer enthusiasts. They are the people who write program notes and the booklets that accompany recordings. They are public and private school music educators and administrators. They are our neighborhood music teachers and the kids who go to them for lessons. They are the writers, readers, and listeners whose musical involvement may mean never playing an instrument or singing a tune. They are college, university, and conservatory students. Our users are people who listen to the radio, have jobs on the radio, read reviews and buy recordings, go to concerts, and download MP3s (sometimes on library workstations). Whether in flesh or in spirit, they are our culture's singers and dancers. In short, our users are much like us.

The Practice of Music Librarianship

Within the library environment, the custody and delivery of music occurs in many ways, and opportunities to work with music in libraries are varied. Cataloging, providing reference assistance, instruction, database design and creation, the management of operations or human resources, and the use and understanding of technology all take on added significance when applied to the delivery of music services because working with music often requires fluency in another language—that of musical notation.

In addition to subject knowledge, catalogers possess sophisticated techniques to make materials in many formats accessible to users. Music reference librarians and catalogers alike are distinctively qualified to interpret musical materials, whether scores, sound recordings, reference books, or electronic databases. Reference librarians are skilled in discerning patrons' needs through artful conversation. Couched in a summary of daily activities is an insightful reminder from reference librarian David Lasocki: "Whether we are figuring out what users need, building relationships, teaching one-on-one, or using our research skills, music reference work is a wonderful training ground for compassion."[6]

To make informed decisions about purchases, those involved in collection development gather information from many sources and review patron requests. Their other activities might include controlling or monitoring a budget, communicating with the library's fiscal officer, developing relationships with commercial vendors and potential donors, and submitting orders for purchase—a task that has been expedited by the welcome aid of technology.

The relationships that music librarians form with their vendors can be particularly congenial, perhaps because they share a love of the subject. Approval plans established with vendors often simplify selection. In the unique case of music, librarians work with their vendors to create appropriate profiles that deliver scores and sound recordings in addition to books.

Those who deal with rare or archival material depend on antiquarian catalogs and their relationships with antiquarian vendors to ensure that they are offered materials fitting their music collection's profile in a timely manner. And since much rare material is also acquired through donation, the music archivist must develop and nurture relationships with potential donors. In this environment, public relations and increasing public awareness of the library's collections go hand in hand with collection development. The music librarian's collection responsibility also involves replacing worn or missing library items and sifting through gift material—"stuff in a box"[7]—to determine its usefulness for the collection. Like all librarians, as budgets dwindle, music librarians continue to seek new means for resource sharing, whether arranging consortial purchases, taking a new look at interlibrary borrowing agreements, or collaborating on the creation of new online and print resources.

Often invisible work ensures the control and accessibility of music resources. Cataloging, binding, marking, repairing, making secure all manner of objects for patrons' use—all these labors, skilled and unskilled, are the province of the music librarian. In some cases, the music librarian is called upon to do them all. Additional activities might include online information service, digitization initiatives, classroom teaching, fundraising, planning special programs or exhibits, and promoting library services among clientele.

One Profession, Many Careers

Those with a serious interest in this profession will find an unparalleled resource in the March 2002 "millenium issue" of *Notes,* the journal of the Music Library Association, which carried thirteen invited essays on the current state of music librarianship. Subsequently reprinted as *Music Librarianship at the Turn of the Century,*[8] the insightful contributions by some of our field's most respected practitioners offer readers an excellent basis for a clear understanding of the field at the present time. While discussing the issues that concern music librarians, the articles also give a sense of career options within the field. Those considering a career in music librarianship will also appreciate the essays in the "American Issue" of *Fontes Artis Musicae,*[9] the journal of the International Association of Music Libraries, compiled to correspond with the recent meeting of IAML in Berkeley, California. In addition, Judith Marley's recent study on education for music librarianship usefully summarizes the history of the profession.[10]

These publications provide a fitting background for the work in hand: a book about careers, which is possible only because of the people whose very careers comprise the profession. This chapter describes a variety of music library environments in stories from the field, told by music librarians doing the work, the few representing the hundreds that this chapter seeks to honor.[11]

Cataloging: "The Guts of Music Librarianship"[12]

"Some people think that catalogers are not public-services oriented," says Cindy Richardson, who catalogs music for the King County Library System in Washington State, "but in my opinion, the best catalogers, whether in academic or public library settings, always keep the end-user in mind." In reflecting on the complex unseen activity that makes library materials accessible to users, Cindy remarks that while a cataloger's work typically begins and ends with the consistent application of cataloging rules governing description and subject access to the materials at hand, there are many decisions along the way that are grounded in the needs and expectations of the population being served. "Catalogers do not have a secret handshake, but those drawn to this aspect of librarianship invariably have a special affinity and aptitude for the work," she says, adding that because a tangible product is involved, successfully balancing the demands of quantity and quality can be challenging.

"Some catalogers have a preference for working with the more scholarly materials that support the curriculum and training needs in universities and conservatories. Others enjoy the diversity and more popular orientation of the materials typically found in public libraries. In either environment," says Cindy, who has worked in both, "there are a few extra dimensions to music cataloging that set it apart from most other cataloging."

Cindy further observes that, when dealing with the basic repertoire of Western art music, music catalogers can expect to encounter multiple manifestations of the same composition, whether as scores or sound recordings. Often the language is other than English, and sometimes reference sources must be consulted to determine the original title of a work, which then serves as the uniform title that brings together all of the different published or recorded versions. Music catalogers must recognize and call attention in the cataloging record to any alterations of the original, such as arrangements or the presence of selections only. For sound recordings, access must be provided for performers as well as composers, and cataloging is usually done in such a way that each piece on a recording may be retrieved individually. While it is certainly possible for nonspecialists to create bibliographic records for music materials, those who specialize in music cataloging rely daily on their academic training in music, and their immersion in music is evident in their work. In keeping with Cindy's initial comment, Mark McKnight, music cataloger at the University of North Texas, places the public service aspect of cataloging at the top of his list of reasons why he likes cataloging music. Mark's "Top Ten" are:

10. Cataloging brings order out of chaos.
9. Cataloging provides intellectual challenges and develops critical-reasoningskills.
8. Cataloging is quantifiable: At the end of the day you can measure how productive (or not) you've been.
7. Contrary to what you might think, cataloging is very much a collaborative effort: you interact with other catalogers andlibrarians, and sometimes even the public!
6. Cataloging teaches you to follow the rules, and lets you be creative when the rules don't fit.
5. Cataloging music exposes you to all kinds of music, some of which you might not otherwise know about, and some you might find you like.
4. Catalogers often have to be detectives, which is sometimes fun, sometimes exasperating.
3. The world of cataloging is constantly changing, with new systems, new rules, new formats and media. There's never a dull moment.
2. Cataloging teaches you to be detail-oriented, but also to look at the larger picture.
1. Cataloging is public service.

Readers of Mark's valuable monograph on music classification[13] will note that he expresses many of Cindy's observations, as does Micki Koth, who works at Yale University. Micki has had a wide range of duties as a library assistant, graduate assistant, and librarian, but finds "none is as fun or as rewarding as cataloging music." Micki sees the challenges in cataloging as "in some ways similar to the challenges of public service. Even though catalogers aren't under pressure to answer a research question with the person standing right there needing an answer for a paper due in two hours, we do have to find answers to questions that are an inevitable part of music cataloging." She also recognizes the necessity of cataloging to make order out of chaos, saying, "Obscure composers and their obscure works that don't appear in the usual reference sources. Russian books about French opera, Macedonian choral music, recordings of Turkish music . . . bringing order to material as diverse as this is a challenge—and is fun," she says, adding, "really," for the unconvinced. "There is great satisfaction in determining what it is that you have and creating a catalog record for it."

Mickey recognizes that part of the enjoyment she derives from her job has to do with where she works. "Having a collection of the quality here at Yale allows me to answer the questions confronting me when I catalog. I appreciate what I have and try to share it with other music catalogers." As a new librarian, Mickey jokingly started the "gin-and-tonic club." She explains, "Someone would ask someone via e-mail to check something in their collection to answer an authority control question. In return, the one doing the favor would receive a drink during the annual MLA meeting. In reality, no one ever kept track. A bunch of catalogers would meet in the bar and buy each other drinks. But it demonstrates the willingness among music catalogers to help each other." Music catalogers repeatedly mention this element of collaboration and support within their community.

Like all catalogers, Micki mentions a healthy respect for the rules, which she admits can seem overwhelming at times. "Add in the knowledge needed of the subject matter and it seems even worse," she goes on. Acknowledging a general perception within librarianship, Mickey observes that "book catalogers and those who catalog in other subject areas view music cataloging as this great big scary thing." Music catalogers see the situation differently. "In reality, it lets me work within a subject area I love—and learn as I work—while using my creativity to do research, and, on top of it, get paid to do it!"

Public Libraries

Among public libraries, which receive their support from city, state, or federal government, one finds a wide range of facilities, from large research libraries in urban settings to modest town libraries. All share a mission of serving the people in the area and are principally supported by tax revenues, though some enjoy the benefit of gifts and endowments. Collections reflect the needs of the community. In large urban libraries, particularly those with a strong research collection, users may be professional musicians and writers as well as enthusiastic amateurs. In contrast, small town libraries might principally support their users' desires for recorded music.

"My situation isn't very typical of most music librarians in public libraries," says Steve Landstreet of the Free Library of Philadelphia, who chairs the Public Libraries Committee of MLA. "We're a bit like NYPL [New York Public Library] in that our music department has fourteen full-time employees and one half-time library assistant. Of those, eight are librarians. There are also three music catalogers." Steve indicates that at this library, much attention is devoted to its special collections. "I work exclusively with music, except when I occasionally sub in the art department," he continues, "but that's only because it's something I enjoy. We don't have a combined department like the Boston or [Washington] DC Public Library—yet!" He alludes to the changes that many libraries are experiencing as downsizing affects their traditional modes of subject-specialized service. Unlike many public libraries, which, Steve says, have abandoned subject divisions in favor of a centralized reference service point, the Free Library of Philadelphia is one that, at this writing, has managed to retain traditional subject divisions.

In many cities, music services are combined with fine arts, dance, recreation, and other "leisure" activities into an inclusive department often staffed by librarians with background in some aspect of the arts. This service model allows for the kind of interdisciplinary immersion that many patrons find satisfying. It also responds to traditionally American biases about "culture" in our society as being synonymous with entertainment, as pastime, as something apart from "work" (traditionally represented by the public library's business department). At the Detroit Public Library, for example, "music reference services are provided by the Music and Performing Arts Department, which also encompasses cinema, theater, radio, television broadcasting, and dance," according to Linda B. Fairtile and Karen M. Burke, in a recent survey.[14] They go on to note that the New Orleans Public Library also "combines music with other subject areas, forming the Periodicals, Arts and Recreation Division," which again reflects the common element of "leisure activities" in this grouping of materials.

"One of the great things about working at a public library reference desk is that you never know what's coming next," Landstreet says. "It might be a rapper who wants to protect his valuable intellectual property and has heard about copyright forms or our music business books, or the guy you thought was going to be that guy turns out to be an aspiring opera and lied singer and is looking for scores or info on competitions."

Unlike the large research library where Steve works, public libraries in small communities and local branches of urban systems are seeing that circulating CD collections make up the bulk of the music materials. In these libraries, limited collections of books and keyboard music often provide a needed supplement to the even more limited musical opportunities in the public schools. And these same libraries offer what might be the last, best hope for the cultivation of a new generation of concertgoers. Librarians who offer music services in the country's public libraries have an opportunity to influence their communities in remarkable ways, as Anna Seaberg found out. Anna selects sound recordings for the King County Library System, which serves the more than forty rural and suburban areas surrounding Seattle. "The kind of selection I do is an interesting mix of reflecting and anticipating people's tastes," she says. "There at least two reasons why people come to the public library: to find the familiar—a known quantity—or to find the unfamiliar—something they've never before encountered. The patrons and I take turns stretching each other. Occasionally, when I've felt that I have really gone out on a limb in the 'spinach music' direction (you know, 'eat this, it's good for you'), I find those can be the titles that generate the most interest."

Anna recalls observing with surprise and satisfaction her patrons' interest in electronic and experimental music, as well as recordings of sub-Saharan pop music and the second Viennese School. She describes her approach to selection: "You try to give people a chance to dip into the Sea of Everything at whatever depth they prefer." She thoughtfully quotes from a note to her library that called "the person who collects and selects [the world music] items" valuable, knowledgeable, and admirable. The grateful patron continued, "I don't speak Oliver [Mtukudzi]'s language but I do listen. His music's rhythm takes me far away."[15]

Tina Murdock, who works at the Dallas Public Library, is responsible for the selection of books about music, recordings, music-related videos, and printed music. An interesting and appealing aspect of Tina's particular job is her service as "the library's liaison to music organizations in the city. That may be my favorite part of the job," she says, "since it gives me a chance to get out and meet musicians doing all kinds of work. Some of them have spent a lifetime helping to build Dallas's cultural environment, and they have invariably been fascinating people who are generous in helping me understand the rich musical heritage of the city."

As traditional headquarters for community educational and cultural events, public libraries also sponsor concert and lecture series. A quick

Google search reveals that libraries in virtually every area of the country are bringing music to the public, through Friends' groups, community arts organizations, or other means. Included in the search results are the Batesville, Indiana, Public Library's "After Hours Concert Series"[16] and the Bastille Day Concert at the Chapel Hill, North Carolina, Public Library, as well as "Concerts from The Library of Congress,"[17] held in what must be regarded as the public library for the nation.

Cathy Dixon works as a librarian/research specialist in the Music Division of the Library of Congress, bringing to her job prior experience as a music librarian and later as chief of the Music Division at the Washington, D.C., Public Library. While many of her responsibilities at the Library of Congress—"handling reference inquiries, using online resources, providing bibliographic instruction, preparing bibliographies/pathfinders, dealing with issues relating to the use of library materials"— are the same she had in her former job at DCPL, she admits that she is awed by the size and strength of the collections and feels privileged to work at LC. But she credits her years at DC Public Library for "the opportunity to be involved with diverse colleagues and clientele" that she knows will "serve her well in any job."

Such opportunities abound in public libraries. "The chance to deal with all types of music and all manner of people can make public librarianship with a music specialty an exciting and rewarding career," says Richard LeSueur, music specialist at the Ann Arbor (MI) District Library. A longtime student of music's place in public libraries, he is careful to point out that except in very large public library systems, "the music librarian is not *just* a music librarian. In some libraries, the holdings and activity in the music collection do not warrant a full-time music staff person." In such libraries, it is not uncommon for other duties such as general reference or cataloging to be part of the position. Richard also observes that in many smaller public libraries, the librarian in charge of the music collection may have no musical background. "This is where those of us with music degrees can be good colleagues," he says with generosity. "We can offer assistance to neighboring institutions."

LeSueur also remarks upon aspects of public library work that provide opportunities for interesting programming: "A series of noontime chamber recitals offers a nice break for the public from harried lunches. A lecture series highlighting an important upcoming musical event can bring the music collection into the public eye. So can creating displays which highlight music in the community." For this music specialist librarian, the joys of reference work in a public library are great: "Finding that song from 1933 for a 70th wedding anniversary, identifying a piece of music that is being whistled over the phone or proving that Aunt Harriet really did sing at the Metropolitan Opera House." The satisfaction in helping "the shy student looking for an audition piece for the school musical or helping a young couple find the perfect music for their wedding can make even the coldest winter day a little nicer."

Music Libraries in Higher Education

Academic Libraries

Within the realm of academic libraries, music services occur in a variety of settings. Often, the placement and custody of music library materials is determined by the size and the academic structure of the institution, political interests, or historical precedent. In the academic environment, several scenarios exist for the provision of music services in libraries.

The Music Branch Library in the Music Department or School

Common to many campuses is the branch music library, which is part of the institution's library system. Usually it is housed within the music department, as is the case at Brown University, St. Olaf College, and the University of Washington, among countless other institutions nationwide.[18] In large music schools the music library itself is a separate building on the campus. The Eastman School of Music at the University of Rochester and Indiana University in Bloomington both boast such facilities.

The special requirements of music study and the special nature of music materials have traditionally determined the necessity for a branch library. Contributing to this administrative model is a widely held belief that a music school's accreditation depends upon an on-site library. In fact, the accreditation guidelines of the National Association of Schools of Music (NASM) simply state that the institution's library must adequately support the programs offered by the institution and be easily accessible to faculty and students.[19]

The Music Department in the Main Campus Library

An interesting variation on the branch music library is the separate music or fine arts department within the main academic library. As in a true branch library, the special nature of music materials justifies keeping them all in the same neighborhood, so that scores and recordings can be consulted together, along with music-specific texts. The fine arts library at Rice University is one such example, with a separate entrance and security gate and its own circulation service point. In these circumstances, it might be quite common for a librarian trained in music to be called upon to field questions outside her area of training. For example, Mary DuMont, the enthusiastic music librarian at Rice University, works alongside a fine arts specialist.

All of Mary's collection development responsibilities are for music. In her library, she tells us, she serves "mostly undergraduate and graduate music students, and music faculty, but I also help a lot of people from the community. I also get a lot of reference questions by phone and e-mail, especially from our music faculty and students, as the music school is on the other side of campus. I get so many of these 'long distance' requests that the typical situation is reversed and the face-to-face questions become the intrusions. I have to work to counteract that feeling—but I really love the fact that my music patrons know who I am and know that I will help them, enough to e-mail or call—and this includes a lot of people I don't know, who get my name from colleagues and friends."

Like many specialist music librarians, Mary works a few hours each week at the main reference desk, where her regular music clientele can also find her. Not surprisingly, she tells us, "At the main reference desk I often deal with totally different questions—lots of science and engineering stuff, and high school students sent by their teachers to do research for school projects. I am also forced to stay in touch with the logistics of library policies to a much greater degree by working at the main reference desk, which is a good thing."

Integrated Music Services in the Main Campus Library

Within the academic setting it is also very common to find music materials among the general collections within the main campus library, where the subject-specialist librarian for music is one with many other subject responsibilities. This librarian might serve at a general reference desk, and select materials for numerous subjects that may be closely related to music like fine arts, theater, film, or dance—or not, depending upon the particular needs of the library and the interests of the music specialist. Music collections in this type of environment are housed alongside other library materials, depending on format. Sound recordings will likely be part of a media center, while print materials logically will be shelved among other subjects. The general reference desk serves all comers, and because the music librarian has many other responsibilities, library users with music needs may not always receive specialized service. In this type of environment, educating one's colleagues is one of the music librarian's jobs. In return, the on-the-job education that the music specialist librarian receives is rewarding in its variety.

"The extensive collections and the larger, more specialized staff [in a large academic library] provide broader and potentially more diverse resources to call upon. Beyond the advantages of having a larger music library/department, usually with more than one music librarian, having subject specialists and extensive collections in related disciplines can provide greater support for interdisciplinary studies," observes Laura K. Probst, former music librarian at the University of Minnesota and now head of Public Services at Penn State University. Noting that specialist librarians in business, social sciences, area studies, foreign languages, and technology all contribute their expertise to the study of music, she also remarks, "While working in a large library provides a wonderful opportunity to specialize in a discipline such as music and to provide resources and services for a focused user group, it also presents a challenge to remain involved in the activities of the larger organization, to watch for opportunities and initiatives that may be beneficial to the users of the music library and to build the collaborative relationships that are so critical to a successful library."

Integrated Music Services in the Media Center

At Emory University[20] Joyce Clinkscales says, "In addition to the music collections, my library houses the audiovisual media for the main library. So we serve not only the music users, but faculty and students from all areas of the arts and sciences. It's a pretty natural combination since all the listening and viewing equipment, plus the expertise to maintain it, can be located in one place. Plus, there's an economy of scale in terms of staffing and hours of operation that we wouldn't have with a separate music library." Joyce's collection includes "visual materials in many different formats, some of which are not standard in the U.S. and some of which are practically obsolete. Our users often need assistance in using these items, and guidance on getting equipment for showing them in classrooms." Her department also runs a booking service for instructors who use visual materials. "Unlike most other library services, the material is guaranteed for a particular date in the future," she says. "It sounds simple, but when several patrons are demanding access within a limited time period, it takes careful monitoring to meet their needs while making sure all reservations are honored as promised." Joyce notes that another aspect of media librarianship involves the licensing and copyright issues peculiar to moving-image materials. And visual materials, especially films, demand considerable maintenance and attention to preservation. "The online-service issues are similar to those for music librarians, with the obvious addition of visual media. And reference service keeps us on our toes, because people come in looking for videos on just about anything."

Departmental Facilities

Not all academic music libraries fall tidily under the administrative umbrella of the campus library system. On most campuses, librarians are aware of proprietary reference collections that exist in one academic department or another. On some campuses, regardless of the music services that are offered formally by the library, the music department supports its own library-like facility. These libraries, listening rooms, or reading rooms, are sometimes staffed by departmental employees, and are usually stocked with materials purchased by the department or donated by faculty and friends, and might house ensemble performance collections, local recital recordings, or more mainstream printed and audiovisual resources. These "guerrilla libraries" can provide trained professional and paraprofessional individuals with opportunities to process materials and serve patrons. The University of Idaho has such a library.[21] In some cases, music departments come to outgrow their departmental libraries and turn to the institution's library system for help or "adoption."

Music Librarians as Teachers

Many academic music librarians spend time in the classroom. Some teach music courses or give instrument instruction. In our complex information environment, most music librarians today teach classes in the use of their libraries' resources. At St. Olaf College, Beth Christensen collaborates with music faculty to create a sequence of course-integrated assignments that build upon one another and directly support and enhance the course content. Of the time and energy it takes to develop these assignments and maintain the program, she says the rewards have been well worth the effort.

Giving basic library instruction to groups of students means better individual questions at the reference desk. Furthermore, Beth points out, it proves to be a cost-effective use of librarians' time and attention. In addition, she has found that her collaborative activity has a direct effect on collection development. "I am better able to anticipate and understand what is needed to support the curriculum by being directly engaged in the teaching process." She goes on to explain that because her students are able to perform independent research and evaluate materials, the St. Olaf faculty have come to expect a high level of critical thinking. Beth considers her collaborative approach essential to the success of the St. Olaf program: "The combined result is much more effective than the services that either the library or the classroom environment could individually provide. The library is an integral part of the music department's goal to educate students as life-long learners and critical thinkers."

One Academic Music Librarian's Career

When mobiblity is possible, music librarianship can offer a fluid, multidimensional career that, over time, encompasses several kinds of jobs. Margaret Erickson, who is in charge of the Art and Music Library at Colby College, has collected and documented Appalachian field recordings, driven a bookmobile in the Blue Ridge Mountains, and worked at the large, research-oriented Enoch Pratt Free Library in Baltimore, "where I learned everything I know about art reference," she says. Her move into academic music librarianship at Ithaca College coincided with the popularity in women's studies that led her to important work in the field of women in music. Along the way, "I did a bit of everything—collections, cataloging, reference," she says. "At Ithaca College, I did more instruction for classes, managerial work, supervising, and planning facilities." This prepared Margaret to lead the Tufts University Music Library, a branch library in a music department. That administrative experience led her to the job she now holds at Colby. "I thought it would be ideal. It combined art and music, and was still administrative." Colby is very small, and now Margaret has many additional responsibilities. But, she says, "I interact with a large cross section of faculty and students. I contribute to general library discussions about electronic resources and interdisciplinary collections. It would take a psychologist to analyze how many parts of my brain are being utilized in this position."

Margaret recognizes that some find it comfortable to specialize in one thing, perhaps because they believe that their music expert knowledge is most suitable or appreciated in the music library setting. "But," she observes, "it is sometimes more exciting to have a wider perspective and multiple subject responsibilities. It expands your lifelong career choices in ways that you may not have anticipated at the beginning of your career."

Conservatory Libraries

Devoted exclusively to the support of performing artists, conservatory libraries are the special libraries of the music world. Jane Gottlieb is the Juilliard School's vice president for library and information resources. Since its founding nearly one hundred years ago, Juilliard has educated some of the world's foremost performing artists. The library and archives collections reflect this distinguished heritage. "Everything that we do here, in collection development as well as in reference work, has a direct relationship to the community's research and performance activities," says Jane. "It is a privilege to serve the Juilliard School community of musicians, dancers, and actors. Indeed, among the many things I love about my job is the opportunity to work with a variety of performing arts disciplines: dancers and actors as well as musicians. In addition to the extensive collections of dance, drama, and music materials, the Juilliard Library maintains a modest-sized but rich collection of general humanities materials to support the research needs of students and faculty for historical and cultural context on the works they are studying." Jane also feels privileged to oversee the school's archives, which will be heavily utilized in Juilliard's upcoming 2005 centennial celebrations.

Bob Follett recently moved from the University of Arizona to the Peabody Conservatory of Music and says he appreciates the difference in reporting structure. Peabody is administratively part of The Johns Hopkins University, but as Bob observes, "the main difference is that at a conservatory (at least here), the library is much more autonomous." At

Peabody, Bob reports to the dean of the Conservatory. "Although we are part of the The Johns Hopkins shared catalog, and are part of the Hopkins Libraries, we are totally funded by the Peabody Institute. In turn, we contribute financially to the shared catalog and to the [extensive] electronic resources available through the catalog." This is partially because of the way Hopkins is organized. "Highly decentralized" is the way Bob describes it. "What I really like most about working for the Conservatory is the 'family atmosphere.' We are physically in a different location from the rest of the University. Being on our own campus makes for much more of a tightly knit group. When you go into the cafeteria for lunch, there are faculty, students and staff all having lunch at the same time. All interactions are much less formal." A conservatory librarian's sense of affiliation is perhaps more certain than that of a music librarian working in a larger library or academic system. Bob says, "I'm never told, 'You're not part of the College of Fine Arts,' because, here, I am part of the Conservatory."

Kathy Abromeit, a reference librarian at the Oberlin Conservatory in Ohio, says sometimes she has to pinch herself to believe that she works in such a place. "The students are highly dedicated and focused, and it is stimulating working with people who are enthusiastic about their art and life. At times, I long for a little complacency, but we don't get that at Oberlin. As with any community that embraces life," Kathy reflects, "there are times that are joyful and then there are disappointments and losses. I'll never forget 9/11 in the Conservatory. Near the end of the day as everyone was walking around in a state of shock, I walked past the orchestra rehearsal room and heard a Mozart symphony floating through the hall. Despite a myriad of feelings that seemed incommunicable, there was voice—the wordless communication of music."

Starting from Scratch: Creating the Special Library

Not long ago, Hollis Near became the first director of Library Services in the ninety-year history of Cornish College of the Arts in Seattle. Cornish, whose enrollment numbers about 650, is one of four arts colleges in the United States that offer programs in both visual and performing arts. Hollis describes the Cornish library as an academic library with a "special library feel," where she is "still plugging holes in basic repertoire for sound recordings and scores." With one other librarian, she has to be "prepared to do just about anything. I like it that way," she says, "because I enjoy both public and technical services."

Her first task was to create a listening center. A grant from the [Paul] Allen Foundation for Music allowed her to boost the compact disc collection and acquire some additional audio equipment, but she also went to secondhand sales to acquire furniture, shelving, and accessories. "Recently a graduating senior thanked me for all the resources he's been able to use in the center," she recalls. "The real payoff was when I heard his excellent composition for string quartet performed later that evening. I realized we had made a difference."

Access to the score collection was still based on a card catalog, so Hollis and her staff took "a year of focused effort to complete a full retrospective conversion of all those records." In the midst of her administrative duties, and coming from a previous job as a selector, Hollis had to learn how to catalog music, attending an OCLC MOUG workshop in Seattle to help her to refine her music cataloging skills.

In July 2003, Cornish College moved into a new building that has tripled the capacity of the library. "I've spent a lot of time working on space plans during the last two years. Because of my acquisitions background, selection continues to be my favorite activity, but with this move I'm excited about the possibilities for expanding reference services and bibliographic instruction," says Hollis. "We all are."

Some Uncommon Settings

Radio and Television Stations

Music librarians at radio and television stations keep track of sizable collections of recordings and quickly process new releases for airplay. At WGBH in Boston, broadcast librarian Alice Abraham assists the on-air staff, who plan programs three months in advance. She also maintains an in-house catalog using FilemakerPro and develops the recording collection. There is only a small acquisition budget, as recordings are mostly acquired by the radio station from recording companies as a promotional service. For this reason, she also works with the record labels, distributors, and artists, not only for acquisition purposes but to arrange promotional efforts including giveaways and station fund-raising premiums. She does reference work for the WGBH staff and also for the listening public and gives public tours of the radio station. "It's a very different situation than being a public or academic librarian," says Alice, who has been profiled in the *Boston Globe*. "I'm the only music librarian at the WGBH Educational Foundation, which has 1,100 employees. Although I work in the Radio Dept, I also assist folks in TV productions, the Caption Center, and other non-broadcast departments." This adds up to a busy and varied workday for this librarian who is also a composer with commissions to her credit.[22]

Larger than most radio stations, WGBH is one of the top five public radio stations in the country. "And we're the most powerful radio station in New England," she goes on, "broadcasting at 100,000 watts. Our WGBH Radio Library has over 80,000 CDs and LP recordings. We're a mixed format station airing classical, jazz, blues, folk/Celtic, and world music. Besides our daily music programs, we produce several national and international programs. We're also known for our frequent studio live performances and concert remotes around New England and beyond."

Abraham adds, "Every day, a new batch of promotional CDs arrives. As the Music Librarian, it's my job to make sure that the new releases are quickly catalogued in our database and made accessible for hosts to use for immediate airplay. I also report what we play to record companies, work with a library assistant on special projects, and supervise four volunteers who do reshelving and data entry."[23]

At many radio stations, the job of music librarian is combined with administrative or broadcasting responsibilities. While there are probably few jobs like the one that Alice describes, work at a radio or television station is an attractive option for someone with the right credentials.

Digital Audio Production and Delivery

The organization of digitized sound is an emerging career option for someone like Jon Haupt, a recent graduate of the Information School at the University of Washington. As part of his master's degree program at the "iSchool," Jon had a directed fieldwork experience at Smithsonian Global Sound,[24] a project affiliated with the Smithsonian Center for Folklife and Cultural Heritage, located in Seattle.[25] Global Sound is intended to be a world music website, seeking to preserve and distribute music from important ethnic sound archives worldwide. At the time of Jon's internship, the six staff members at Global Sound were the director, the project manager, a technical director, an ethnomusicologist, a cataloger, and a sound editor.

Under the direction of Susan Golden, project manager, Jon says, "I did two hundred hours of work, about two thirds of which were spent on cataloging-related tasks, among them descriptive cataloging of sound recordings, maintaining and selecting terms from controlled vocabularies, and writing definitions of instruments, genres, culture groups, and other terms for a glossary. Another large chunk of my time was spent working on the search requirements document for the project website with Susan Golden." For Jon it was a great experience to be involved with the company in its early stages of development, learning both technical and managerial skills. Jon also participated in discussions that involved usability and appearance of the Global Sound website's search and browse pages.

Sound recordings in Global Sound's database require detailed description beyond AACR2 practices, so Global Sound has created its own cataloging tool. Since users will be able to access music at the "track" level rather than the "container," or album, level, each track has several relevant pieces of information attached to it for description and access. Susan Golden, who directed Jon's internship, explains that the cataloging tool uses a very detailed authority file created by and for the project.[26]

Haupt concludes, "As an intern at Global Sound, I increased my knowledge of cataloging, authority control, web and interface design, and project management. I highly recommend such a job for information professionals who are interested in music but not interested in working in a traditional library setting."

Susan Golden observes that online audio delivery is a growing professional field, attracting people from the music industry, from business, and from radio, for example, who are returning to school for the kind of training that will position them for new jobs. "This kind of work environment requires a very flexible individual," she says. As project manager for Global Sound, Susan works in every aspect of the site's development. She comes from a background that has ranged from African studies to storytelling, through libraries (where she specialized at different times in children's services, music, and business), to web development and the dot-com phenomenon. With obvious appreciation, Golden says that she's come full circle to find herself involved in the delivery of world music to today's consumers. "In the web world, where small teams 'do everything,' there's often a disconnect between the technicians and the content experts," she says. "In our operation we try to bridge that gap." As Jon noted, diverse groups constantly discuss the project to determine the next step. To support its growing and detailed catalog, Global Sound is developing its own authority files, necessary for the levels of description involved. "The people who succeed in this kind of work are those who possess an innate ability for structure along with a willingness to break the rules," Susan says.

Since Global Sound is intended as a commercial product, part of Susan's job is making sure that its information is musically and culturally accurate, and that it is as useful as it is attractive. "One day, I could be talking to a tester, another a developer, and the one after that, a musician." It's important for her to know every aspect of the project, and to be able to relate them to one another. She cautions that building something from the ground up can be as uncomfortable as it is exciting. But it is the excitement of the Global Sound project that Susan enthusiastically communicates. Her passion is evident when she talks about making available the vast resources of the world's musical legacies.

Sound Archives

The Institute of Jazz Studies is the world's foremost jazz archive and research facility. As part of the Rutgers University Libraries, the Institute is used by students from Rutgers—especially those in the new master's program in jazz history and research. The Institute also serves other institutions, teachers, scholars, authors, independent researchers, musicians, the media, record companies, libraries and other archives, and arts agencies.[27]

At the Institute of Jazz Studies, Vincent Pelote is head of Special Collections and sound archivist. As such, he is responsible for purchasing books, CDs, DVDs, and other materials for the collection and for sending those books to be cataloged by the Rutgers University Libraries. Special skills as a sound archivist enable Vincent to care properly for the recordings, particularly 78s and LPs, cleaning them when necessary and rehousing them in proper sleeves and containers. He also repairs broken open reel tape, adding leader tape when required, making sure the tape is wound properly on its reel, and maintains all of the Institute's playback equipment: turntables, amplifiers, cassette decks, and other audio media. "I am also in charge of the IJS sound lab," Vincent writes. "We reformat old and deteriorating items onto a sturdier analog or digital medium." The archive is used by working musicians as well as scholars. About serving the jazz community, Vincent recalls, "I'll never forget meeting Mel Torme when he returned some borrowed materials to the archives."

An active member of ARSC (The Association for Recorded Sound Collections), Vincent has served the organization in many capacities.

"Dedicated to research, study, publication, and information exchange surrounding all aspects of recordings," ARSC supports librarians and archivists' work and also attracts a wide membership that includes historians and collectors as well as people in the music industry.[28] Vincent currently chairs the organization's Discography Committee. "One of the things we hope to do is formulate guidelines for discographies that will be submitted to the *ARSC Journal*," he says. He also co-chairs the committee that selects commendable books and liner notes as recipients of the ARSC Award for Excellence.

Vincent is a jazz guitarist who each winter conducts the MLA Big Band, a formidable pickup ensemble of MLA members who gather to entertain at the annual conference of the Music Library Association. "I do a jazz radio show called 'Jazz From the Archives,'[29] where the staff take turns hosting," he says, disclosing an interesting and perhaps unseen aspect of his work with his collections. "One of my greatest moments was when I had the pleasure of doing a show with one of my favorite guitar players, Remo Palmier."

Ensemble Libraries

One of the most specialized settings for music collections and services is the performance library. Serving such organizations as a symphony, opera or ballet orchestra, or major concert band, the librarian often presides over "the hub of organizational activities for the entire orchestra."[30] Along with its extensive collection of performance scores and parts, the performance library often includes reference materials to assist in programming. Librarians in these facilities have the opportunity to work closely with conductors and instrumentalists, as well as those responsible for programming. In addition to the unusual responsibility of marking scores according to conductors' specifications, these librarians assist writers of program notes with research and may participate in planning concerts. In 1983 the Major Orchestra Librarians' Association was founded "with the aim of improving communication among orchestra librarians." Today an international organization, MOLA offers education, networking, and support for its members.

Jane Cross is a music librarian who began her career with the US Marine Band as a staff sergeant after completing her bachelor's in music and English. She has since been promoted to the rank of GySgt (Gunnery Sergeant) and has completed her MLS. "Working in this library is similar to working in a symphony orchestra library in that we are primarily performance oriented, and indeed we are members of MOLA," Jane says. "Yet we also maintain a small reference collection and a variety of archival materials, and in that way we share many of the same concerns as librarians affiliated with MLA. The staff here estimates that this library is one of the largest performing libraries in the world with approximately 50,000 titles of scores for band, orchestra, small ensembles, and piano/vocal."

The mission of the band, which has long been known as "The President's Own," is to provide music for the president of the United States and the commandant of the Marine Corps, but the work of the band and its busy librarian is far from simple. The library provides music for the many ensembles that comprise the US Marine Band, keeping folders at the ready for ensembles to go to the White House at a moment's notice, which they do approximately 300 times a year to provide music for state occasions. The library also serves the band that provides music for funerals at Arlington National Cemetery and ceremonies in the Washington, D.C. area. "In addition to this ever-changing schedule," Jane continues, "we provide a public concert series from January through May in various concert halls in the metropolitan area. During the summer the band performs twice a week on the National Mall, and during the fall a concert band tours a section of the United States, while at home there is a chamber music series and an educational outreach program known as Music in the Schools. As you can see, music preparation is an ongoing duty, as is preparation of the band's printed programs." The library is also frequently called upon to verify, research, or support research related to the history of the band. This includes "providing information about our seventeenth Director, John Philip Sousa." The library's collections of photographs, uniforms, correspondence, clippings, manuscripts, and other memorabilia are unusual and valuable resources. "In the meantime," says Jane, "we're getting ready for a move to a new library, developing a new version of our automated catalog, and transitioning to a new, Navy-mandated computing environment. All of these tasks, and more, are handled by a staff of six librarians."

With so much variety, Jane says appreciatively that the job is never boring. "In one day I may handle reference-type questions, prepare music, catalog, troubleshoot technology issues, and license music for an upcoming recording." Librarians also go with the band and orchestra to performances to handle the music and assist the ensemble as needed. As part of her work Jane has had the privilege of attending such events as the White House Millennium Ball, the NATO 50th Anniversary Ceremony, and the 2001 Presidential Inauguration, as well as numerous White House Easter Egg Roll events, July 4th celebrations, and holiday receptions. She also traveled with the band to Lucerne, Switzerland, to support the band's performances for the 2001 WASBE (World Association of Symphonic Bands and Ensembles) Conference.

Among her poignant memories, Jane counts setting up the band on the White House South Lawn in the chilly dawn hours one October morning, "which happened to be my birthday. We were there to play for a surprise birthday event for Hillary Clinton's birthday. As the band played 'Happy Birthday,' I watched the sun rise through the mist over the Ellipse."

Jane also recalls standing on the South Lawn a few years later in a pouring rain, "talking to two nice young ladies who happened to walk up." They were waiting to find out if the band would play in the rain for the annual 4th of July celebration. The girls eventually went into the White House to dry off and the band was told to pack up. "It wasn't until later that I realized I had been talking not to interns or social aides, but to President Bush's daughters." So far, says music librarian GySgt Jane Cross, "it has been an amazing career, and I can't wait to see what's next."

Community

In these profiles of music librarians and their work there is a strong unifying element. Leslie Bennett, music librarian at the University of Oregon, has observed that although other professionals usually acquire their subject knowledge and sometimes their job skills through postsecondary education, most music librarians are likely to have begun their musical training as younger people. She defines the distinctive group of librarians in which she finds herself by saying, "We've learned a special language in music that not everyone has. Most of us learned it early on and have grown up with it. We've lived with our subject our whole lives."[31]

This lifelong involvement with the subject transcends the workplace. In the original version of *Careers in Music Librarianship*, Lenore Coral wrote that "the profession of music librarian seems to have some unique qualities. Its members often find great camaraderie in its ranks and a feeling of great satisfaction with their work."[32] Years later, these personal vignettes substantiate her observation. Most important, even as they serve to illustrate the characteristics of the profession, these stories demonstrate that the "unique qualities" are, in fact, in the people who bring the profession to life.

Notes

1. Alexander Hyatt King, "The Music Librarian and His Tasks, National and International," *Fontes Artis Musicae,* 6 (1959), 49–55, reprinted in *Reader in Music Librarianship,* ed. Carol June Bradley (Washington, DC: Microcard Editions Books, 1973), 316.

2. Lenore Coral, "Music Librarianship," in *Careers in Music Librarianship: Perspectives from the Field,* comp. Carol Tatian, MLA Technical Report, 18. (Canton, MA: Music Library Association, 1990), 3.

3. Ivan Hewett, "The Great Divide,"*BBC Music Magazine* (January 2003): 28–30.

4. Deborah Campana, "Music Supporting Comprehensive Schools of Music,"*Fontes Artis Musicae* 48, no. 4 (October–December 2001): 353.

5. Michael Gorman, *Our Singular Strengths: Meditations for Librarians.* (Chicago: American Library Association, 1998): 3.

6. "Music Reference as a Calling," *Notes* 56, no. 4 (June 2000): 892.

7. Phrase coined by Suki Sommer, remembered by the author.

8. *Music Librarianship at the Turn of the Century,* ed. Richard Griscom. MLA Technical Reports no. 27. Lanham, MD: Scarecrow, 2000. First published as special issue of *Notes* 56, no. 3 (March 2000).

9. *Fontes Artis Musicae* 48, no. 4 (October–December 2001). Daniel Zager, guest editor.

10. Judith L. Marley,"Education for Music Librarianship Within the United States: Needs and Opinions of Recent Graduate/Practitioners," *Fontes Artis Musicae* 49, no. 3 (July/September 2002): 139–72.

11. Throughout this chapter, unless otherwise noted, quotations and allusions to remarks by practicing music librarians are derived—sometimes verbatim—from personal e-mail correspondence with the author during the spring of 2003, printed with their knowledge and their understanding of the chapter's informal nature. To all of my music-librarian colleagues who offered their thoughts goes my heartfelt appreciation for their collaborative spirit and good will.—P. E.

12. Phrase coined by Harold Samuel, remembered by Michelle Koth.

13. Mark McKnight, *Music Classification Systems.* MLA Basic Manual Series, no.1. Series Ed. Jean Morrow. (Lanham, MD: Scarecrow, 2002).

14. Linda B. Fairtile and Karen M. Burke, "Music Collections in American Public Libraries," *Fontes Artis Musicae* 48, no. 4 (October–December 2001): 338.

15. Anonymous quotation provided by Anna Seaberg.

16. Batesville Memorial Public Library, www.bmpl.cnz.com/after.html (15 April 2003).

17. "Concerts from the Library of Congress," www.loc.gov/rr/perform/concert/1997–98/contents.html (15 April 2003).

18. Respectively, www.brown.edu/Facilities/University_Library/libs/orwig/orwigtext.html, www.stolaf.edu/library/libs, www.lib.washington.edu/music/reference.html (13 April 2003).

19. National Association of Schools of Music, *2001–2002 Handbook* (Reston, VA: NASM, 2001), 64.

20. http://web.library.emory.edu/libraries/music/ (27 June 2003).

21. www.uidaho.edu/LS/Music/schuldt.html (15 May 2003).

22. Mark Feeney, "Plenty of Shelf Life at This Radio Station," *Boston Globe* third edition (September 16, 2002), B7.

23. Alice Abraham, "The WGBH Radio Library," http://wgbh.org/article?item_id=191752&parent_id=191736 (1 April 2003).

24. www.globalsound.org.

25. This section is derived from Jon Haupt's unpublished report, "Directed Fieldwork at Smithsonian Global Sound," prepared in the fall of 2002.

26. Telephone interview with Susan Golden, May 2003.

27. From the Institute of Jazz Studies' website, www.libraries.rutgers.edu/rul/libs/jazz/jazz.shtml, accessed as www.libraries.rutgers.edu/rulib/abtlib/danlib/jazz.htm (23 May 2003).

28. ARSC website, www.arsc–audio.org/ (25 May 2003).

29. "Jazz From the Archives," a weekly radio program heard on Sunday at 11pm on WBGO–88.3 FM, Newark. http://wbgo.org/ (5 May 2003)

30. Quotations in this paragraph are from the Major Orchestra Librarians' Association, "The Orchestra Librarian, A Career Introduction," www.mola-inc.org/orchlib.html (3 April 2003).

31. Personal conversation, May 2003.

32. Coral, "Music Librarianship," 30.

2

Preparing to
Be a Music Librarian

Jean Morrow

Music librarians come in many varieties, as do their job responsibilities and the types of experience and knowledge they bring to their jobs. The typical music librarian comes to the profession already possessing a strong background in music and has learned about library procedures in library school, on the job, or, in the majority of cases, through a combination of both. One can travel many routes to become a competent music librarian. Some of the most renowned members of this profession spent years working as musical scholars, others as performing musicians, often coming only later in their careers to library work. Among younger members of the profession, many decided early in their college years that they wanted to combine their love of music and musical training with library work and earned degrees in both fields before ever seeking professional employment.

Academic Qualifications

To succeed in today's competitive job market, an aspiring music librarian almost always needs to acquire degrees in both music and library science. Employers occasionally accept equivalent experience or knowledge in lieu of one of those degrees but have done so much less frequently in

recent years. Depending on the position, a bachelor's degree with a
concentration in music may suffice to fulfill the necessary music
requirements. Library degrees are only offered at the graduate level,
however, and for the most part can only be earned at large universities.[1]
The ideal library school program for music librarianship offers the
opportunity to learn about all aspects of administering a music library,
develops skills in using music reference materials, and teaches the
elements of bibliographic control of music. Approximately fifty accredited
universities in the United States and Canada offer courses or training
related to music library work, but the scope of training offered for music
librarianship varies widely among those institutions.[2]

Six universities currently offer joint master's degree programs in
which the student may earn both the master's degree in library science
and a master's degree in music simultaneously. At these universities, the
library schools and the music schools offer separate instruction and
separate degrees. The student enrolled in a joint degree program takes a
core of music courses, a core of library science courses, music
bibliography, music librarianship, and some type of internship in a music
library setting, and usually undertakes a thesis or bibliographic project.

Although only a small number of universities offer the joint degree
program in music librarianship, additional schools offer a concentration
in music librarianship. Courses in these programs include music
librarianship, music cataloging, and music bibliography. Many more
universities offer a course in music librarianship or the opportunity to
take an internship or practicum in music librarianship. Over forty
universities will transfer credit from the music department to the library
degree for specific courses such as music bibliography.

Courses in music librarianship vary somewhat in content among
universities, depending on the emphasis of the individual instructor. Some
of the courses focus on reference materials, others on library
administration. Some cover both of these topics and also include the
principles of music cataloging.

In the great majority of music library positions, a solid grounding in
music reference materials and music bibliography will be necessary.
Music librarians not only need to know how to find music information
efficiently themselves but also need to be able to instruct others in using
reference tools and conducting research. The library school student who
has only studied music at the undergraduate level should make every
effort to take some type of music bibliography course, if not in the library

degree program then in the music department. If neither of these options is available, an independent study or practicum might provide in-depth work with reference resources.

Students who aspire to work in academic library settings should also plan to undertake additional music study at the graduate level, preferably in music history or musicology. Because academic librarians spend much of their time assisting students and faculty with the resources that support the academic curriculum, they should possess a fairly comprehensive knowledge of music history and the published literature in this field. It is certainly possible to acquire this knowledge independent of formal graduate study, but meeting an employer's requirements for an academic position will be difficult without the actual graduate degree.

In addition to acquiring a solid grounding in music literature and reference materials, the future librarian needs to become familiar with the basic workings of a music library and the many issues that are unique to administering music collections. The more that can be learned during library school study, the easier will be the student's transition into a first professional position. Often library students have already had the advantage of music library work prior to or during their library degree work. These students are especially fortunate if they can work under the mentorship of an experienced music librarian. Such work settings usually provide the best opportunities for learning the workings of a music library and becoming familiar with standard collection materials.

Knowledge of Collection Materials

Music librarians universally have been drawn to their profession by their deep enthusiasm for music and draw much of their enjoyment at work simply by being able to handle music materials and assist in making them available to other musicians and music lovers. It is generally expected that a trained musician will bring to library work a basic familiarity with the standard repertoire, musical styles and genres, and the variety of formats in which music is made available. Traditionally, music collections have included published literature in the areas of music history, ethnomusicology, theory, and music education. More recently, library collections have broadened their scopes beyond the standard Western classical repertoire in order to support the widening interests of musicians and scholars in the music of non-Western cultures and in areas of study introduced by the "new musicology" such as gender studies, popular music, and music for "other purposes."[3]

Knowledge of the standard repertoire, music literature, and music reference materials provides the foundation for success in all music library work and is essential to fulfilling job responsibilities in reference, cataloging, and collection management. The core reference and research materials found in the standard music collection include both print and electronic publications of general and specialized encyclopedias and dictionaries, bio-bibliographies, subject bibliographies, music bibliographies, periodical indexes, thematic catalogues, discographies, the core journal titles, major collected editions of composers, scholarly anthologies, music facsimiles, and the standard historical and theoretical texts.

The music librarian has to become familiar with all of these basic collection tools and utilize them efficiently and appropriately. To provide effective reference service, the librarian needs to evaluate the contents of these resources as to their appropriateness for a particular situation and to provide accurate answers with the resources on hand. The cataloger relies on these resources to assist in the bibliographic description of music materials, establishing name headings and titles and determining their publication histories. The collection manager uses these same tools to evaluate collections and assist in the acquisitions process.

Knowledge of Music Library Functions

Library school education today is designed to equip the student with the necessary skills and knowledge to meet the challenges of working in the 21st century library. But those preparing to work in music libraries will encounter unique issues in dealing with music materials, most especially in their cataloging, their conservation, their shelving, and their use. Even the most educated of musicians will require several years of experience to learn how to manage music collections in a manner that makes them easily accessible and provides for their long-term preservation.[4]

Although only a minority of librarians will actually be required to catalog music materials, every music librarian should acquire a solid grasp of the principles of music cataloging. The music librarian needs to be familiar with the major music classification schemes and understand their structure in order, at the very least, to know how collections are organized and to locate materials quickly on the shelves. The librarian must be familiar with the elements of bibliographic description to be able to identify what formats and editions are represented in the bibliographic record. In order to be able to search the catalog efficiently for music, the librarian needs to understand the principles for constructing uniform titles and the structure of Library of Congress Subject Headings for music. The librarian also needs to understand how automated systems handle music.

Those who are interested in music cataloging as a profession, however, would benefit most from an actual course in the subject. More often than not, the music cataloger has to learn the principles of cataloging music formats on the job and, hopefully, under the guidance of an experienced practitioner. Very often, music librarians find themselves in a library without a music cataloging professional and become the final authority on questions relating to the cataloging of the collection's music even though the general catalogers do the actual cataloging.

Equally as important as providing access to the materials, a music librarian must know how to care for them. The majority of printed music comes to the library requiring some type of binding in order to survive normal wear and tear from performing musicians. Librarians must be informed about binding procedures, paper types, conservation practices, and shelving options. Often they find themselves giving direction to the general bindery staff, to commercial binders, and to the publishers who provide the music scores and parts.

Audiovisual materials also require proper care and shelving to ensure easy access and long-term preservation. Music librarians must know how to select and maintain the appropriate equipment for audiovisual collections and the requirements of the different recording formats. In administering an audiovisual collection, the librarian frequently has to deal with facility issues—how best to outfit the library for the playback of these materials.

Perhaps more than any other library professional, the music librarian has to be knowledgeable about the copyright law. Music librarians at many institutions often find themselves to be the last word on questions of copyright, probably because they deal with it in so many different situations. Within the library itself, copyright law affects the library's preservation policies, acquisitions decisions, and digitization projects. The librarian must take responsibility for the collection materials being used in accordance with copyright law when patrons photocopy print materials, dub sound recordings, or photocopy and digitize materials for class reserves.

Nonmusical Knowledge and Skills

Success in the field of music librarianship requires not only comprehensive subject knowledge of music and music library functions but also additional knowledge and skills that would be welcome in any library setting but are essential in working with music collections. Foremost for the music librarian is a familiarity with other languages. Much of the vocal music in library collections includes non-English text. Many music publications require bibliographic knowledge of European languages in order to read their title pages or labels. A large percentage of the basic reference and bibliographic tools, as well as many music journals and much of the published literature on music, are written in other languages.

In addition to language skills, knowledge of related subjects such as dance and art can be helpful to music librarians, especially those whose patrons are working in interdisciplinary studies. Many positions in fine arts departments, in particular, require the librarian to oversee the music as well as the art and/or possibly the dance collections. Strong music qualifications are usually preferred for these positions, but the candidate who also has a background in art and/or dance will have an added advantage in competing for these positions and fulfilling their job responsibilities.

The music librarian will also make good use of communication skills and teaching ability. Librarians who have come to their work with teaching experience find a perfect outlet for their skills. In particular, the librarian will be asked to instruct patrons individually on the effective use of collection materials and, in academic settings, often assist with classroom instruction on library use.

Finally, the music librarian needs to become proficient with technology and be up to date with all hardware and software developments that serve as the foundation for library service.

Summary of Core Competencies

The breadth of knowledge and number of skills required by the music specialist may seem staggering to the beginning student, but keep in mind that no one arrives at a first professional job with every necessary tool under his or her belt. Despite their best efforts at preparing to be a music librarian, most professionals find themselves continuing to learn at their work for many years. Those who find employment with more specialized collections may have little preparation for their specific job duties. Apart from the more common situations of public and academic collections, librarians may work with archives and special collections, with performance collections, with radio collections, or in television and film libraries. All of these positions will require special skills and knowledge that, more often than not, only get learned on the job.

For many years the Music Library Association has contemplated the establishment of standards for music librarianship that could be used both by library schools responsible for educating and training future music librarians as well as by those wanting to prepare themselves to work in the profession. Much has been written on this topic, but to date no standards have been formally adopted. One of the obstacles in setting standards for library schools has been the issue of credit hours—library school administrations are reluctant to allocate more than a small number of credits to music librarianship studies. Without the benefit of formal standards, the burden for deciding what and how to teach library students continues to fall directly on the shoulders of the individual music librarians who are teaching in library school programs.

In lieu of adopting a formal set of standards, the Music Library Association recently developed a set of core competencies for music librarians. These competencies are included in a paper on this topic prepared by David Hunter on behalf of the association's Library School Liaison Subcommittee. The complete set of competencies is included here to serve as a guide for all those who aspire to become successful music librarians.[5]

The Core Competencies of Music Librarians

Professional Ethos
Music librarians:
1.1. Work to advance the goals of their employing organizations;

1.2. Recognize the diversity of musics, library users (the client group), staff and the wider community, and encourage all in their musical endeavors and enquiries;
1.3. Are committed to excellence in all areas of service;
1.4. Continually assess the effectiveness of provided and potential materials and services;
1.5. Are effective communicators;
1.6. Participate in the professional community.

Training and Education
Music librarians have:
2.1. Course work at the higher education level in music;
2.2. The ability to read music;
2.3. Education at the graduate level in library and information science;
2.4. Knowledge of a language in addition to English;
2.5. Experience as a performing artist;
2.6. Familiarity with a variety of research methods.

Reference and Research
Music librarians:
3.1. Are highly knowledgeable concerning the content of information resources in any format;
3.2. Are highly knowledgeable concerning information access;
3.3. Develop and employ a variety of information delivery systems, as appropriate to each user;
3.4. Constantly evaluate the quality of information sources;
3.5. Create indexes, catalogs, finding aids, brochures, exhibitions, and bibliographies (whether print or electronic) to enhance access to local collections or to a body of music or music literature;
3.6. Provide accurate answers (within the limits of the source materials).

Collection Development
Music librarians:
4.1. Develop collections to meet the needs of users (both present and future) regardless of format;
4.2. Keep abreast of changes in the artistic, business, scholarly, and publishing aspects of music;
4.3. Improve the capability of the library by obtaining access to remote databases;
4.4. Ensure sufficient funds are available for acquisition and preservation of materials;
4.5. Maintain strong ties with vendors;
4.6. Evaluate individual items in collections for continuing relevance;

4.7. Participate in digitization projects to ensure the long-term preservation and wider dissemination of material.

Collection Organization
Music librarians:
5.1. Ensure that materials are housed and organized to meet the needs and expectations of users and organizations;
5.2. Ensure that cataloguing and/or listing meets applicable standards;
5.3. Participate in the sharing of catalog data;
5.4. Ensure that users have appropriate access to materials;
5.5. Ensure that users have access to catalog data;
5.6. Work to improve library data systems, with a goal of integrating circulation, acquisition, and catalog information.

Library Management
Music librarians:
6.1. Control the budget for all aspects of their libraries, including staff, acquisitions, maintenance, and information and audio technology;
6.2. Create both short and long term plans to ensure optimal use of facilities, materials and services, and provide the necessary vision for accomplishing change;
6.3. Hire, train, supervise, and evaluate staff in an environment of trust and respect;
6.4. Ensure that staff continue to receive training by providing access to continuing education and other opportunities for improving skills and knowledge;
6.5. Identify and obtain sources of funding, both from within and outside of the organization;
6.6. Provide leadership not only within the library but also in terms of information provision to the organization of which their library is a part;
6.7. Seek partnerships within and without the organization that will assist with accomplishing missions and goals;
6.8. Ensure that there are no barriers to access.

Information and Audio Technology and Systems
Music librarians:
7.1. Are familiar with developments in hardware, software, and networking, and the integration of systems and media;
7.2. Recommend, plan, implement, and evaluate the installation of relevant information and audio technology and systems;
7.3. Use information and audio technology to enhance services and information delivery.

Teaching
Music librarians:
8.1. Educate users (actual, virtual, and potential), administrators, and
      donors through all appropriate means, including paper, e-mail,
      websites, classes, demonstrations, presentations, individual
      consultation, radio, television, recordings, performances, exhibits;
8.2. Work with faculty and teachers, performers, and listeners to design
      curricula and assignments that are effective, to create interesting
      performances, and to aid lifelong learning;
8.3. Promote the effective use of all technologies;
8.4. Provide guidance on the materials, services, and information to
      which users have access.

Suggestions for Further Reading

Cherubini, Timothy, J., comp. and ed. *Directory of Library School
      Offerings in Music Librarianship*, 7th ed. Canton, MA: Music Library
      Association, 1998. Also available at www.musiclibraryassoc.org/
      services/se_schoo.htm.
Hunter, David. "Core Competencies and Music Librarians." Prepared
      on behalf of the Music Library Association's Library School Liaison
      Subcommittee. Available on the MLA website at
      www.musiclibraryassoc.org/pdf/Core_Competencies.pdf.
Marley, Judith L. "Education for Music Librarianship within the United
      States: Content Analysis of Selected Documentation and Structured
      Interviews with Selected Practitioners." Ph.D. diss., University of
      Pittsburgh, 2000.
Morrow, Jean. "Education for Music Librarianship." *Notes* 56 (2000):
      655–61.
Ochs, Michael. "A Taxonomy of Qualifications for Music Librarianship:
      The Cognitive Domain." *Notes* 33 (1976): 27–44.
"Qualifications of a Music Librarian." Written on behalf of the Music
      Library Association's Committee on Professional Education by Linda
      I. Solow, Susan T. Sommer, and D. W. Krummel, chair. Published in
      several journals, including *Journal of Education for Librarianship*
      16 (1974): 53–59.
Roberts, Don L. "Education for Music Librarians in the United States
      and Canada." *Fontes Artis Musicae* 32 (1985): 59–62. (Updates
      Young's 1984 article on this topic.)

Solow, Linda I. "Education for Music Librarians in the United States and Canada." *Fontes Artis Musicae* 26 (1979): 44–47. (Paper also delivered at IAML 1976 Conference in Bergen, at the session sponsored by the Commission on Education and Training.)

Tatian, Carol, comp. *Careers in Music Librarianship: Perspectives from the Field.* MLA Technical Report, 18. Canton, MA: Music Library Assocation, 1990.

Young, Bradford. "Education for Music Librarianship." *Notes* 40 (1984): 510–28.

Notes

1. Simmons College in Boston remains the only small college offering a library degree through its Graduate School of Information and Library Science.

2. For several decades, the Music Library Association has compiled a comprehensive listing of available programs in its *Directory of Library School Offering in Music Librarianship.* The directory describes programs alphabetically by institution and includes indexes by categories of what is offered: joint degree programs, concentrations in music librarianship, individual courses, and/or internships and practica.

3. There is a wealth of published literature describing the basic materials of music library collections. For a basic overview, consult the bibliographies for this author's course on music librarianship at Simmons College, http://websimmons.edu~morrow/435.html (8 September 2003), or Mary Wallace Davidson's Seminar in Music Librarianship at Indiana University, www.musicindiana.edu/muslib/L631 (8 September 2003).

4. The Music Library Association Basic Manual Series will be of special interest to any newcomer to the profession. Published by Scarecrow Press, the series to date includes *Music Classification Systems* by Mark McKnight and *Binding and Care of Printed Music* by Alice Carli. Forthcoming manuals will treat the topics of reference, library instruction, acquisitions, media equipment, and performance libraries.

5. The entire paper is available on the Music Library Association website at www.musiclibraryassoc.org/pdf/Core_Competencies.pdf (8 September 2003).

3

What Employers Want Now:
A Survey of the MLA Job List

Renée McBride

Positions that combine music and library expertise exist in a variety of institutions, businesses, and organizations. They offer an array of types of work and vary in their expectations and requirements. The purpose of this chapter is to inform those preparing for a career in music librarianship or seeking music library employment of the various opportunities available and the qualifications needed to pursue these opportunities.

A portion of this information was compiled for a presentation at the Personnel Subcommittee's "Interview Workshop" at MLA's 2002 Annual Meeting. For that presentation, as MLA's placement officer, I surveyed job postings in MLA's *Placement Service Job List* from January 1999 though December 2001. For the present publication, the survey has been extended through April 2003. Unlike most content analyses of job announcements, neither a literature review nor a statistical analysis is presented here. This report focuses solely on music librarianship, outlining the types of hiring institutions and library positions represented in the *Placement Service Job List*, briefly describing the responsibilities of the various positions, and explaining the qualifications needed to fulfill these responsibilities. The chapter concludes with a list of recent publications and current resources that may be useful to job seekers.

This survey of the *Placement Service Job List* from January 1999 through April 2003 includes a total of 365 positions, excluding MLA organizational positions, positions that were reposted, and those that were clerical in nature or did not necessarily require library expertise (e.g., fellowship applications). The types of institutions advertising in the *Placement Service Job List* and the number of ads posted by each type during this period are as follows, listed in descending order of number of postings:

- Academic libraries: 228
- Public libraries: 51
- Conservatories: 22
- Orchestras: 11
- Government libraries: 11
- Cataloging services: 10
- Special libraries and organizations: 8
- Publishers and dealers: 7
- Museums: 7
- Independent archives: 6
- School libraries: 3
- Opera libraries: 1

The types of positions advertised by these various hiring institutions breaks down as follows, again listed in descending order of number of postings:

Academic Libraries

- Music librarian: 85
- Cataloger: 44
- Performing arts/audiovisual (AV) librarian: 33
- Reference: 26
- Technology/media: 17
- Archivist: 11
- Technical services: 5
- Collection development/bibliographer: 4
- Music department librarian: 3

Public Libraries

- Cataloger: 20
- Reference: 15
- Music librarian: 10
- Performing arts librarian: 2

- Project manager: 2
- Collection development: 1
- Video specialist: 1

Conservatories

- Music librarian: 10
- Cataloger: 10
- Archivist: 1
- Performing arts librarian: 1

Orchestras

- Intern: 6
- Assistant librarian: 2
- Head librarian: 1
- Executive director: 1
- Information resource associate: 1

Government Libraries

- Cataloger: 5
- Music librarian/reference: 5
- Unknown: 1

Cataloging Services

- Scores and AV/"multiple formats": 6
- Sheet music: 4

Special Libraries and Organizations

- Reference, collection development, website maintenance, research, interlibrary loan, authority work: 1
- Arts administration: 1
- Editing of abstracts: 1
- Research: 1
- Music transcription and engraving, contract negotiation, public relations, collection development: 1
- Cataloging and reference: 1
- Research and funding coordinator: 1
- Librarian: 1

Publishers and Dealers

- Orchestral music rental librarian: 1
- Administrative assistant: 1
- Production assistant: 1
- Associate director, library/studio administrator: 1
- Website editor : 1
- Assistant: 1
- Project officer: 1

Museums

- Information specialist: 3
- Media archives assistant: 1
- Cataloger: 1
- Curator/librarian: 1
- Curator/scholar: 1

Independent Archives

- Audio preservationist: 2
- Curator: 1
- Archive librarian: 1
- Associate library director: 1
- Assistant archivist: 1

School Libraries

- Music librarian/instrument and equipment manager: 3

Opera Libraries

- Tape librarian/archivist: 1

With this overview of the music library job market in place, what follows is a summary of the qualifications which, at this writing, are sought by hiring institutions for their various positions, and how they relate to the activities that take place in different music library positions.

First and foremost, an American Library Association (ALA) accredited library degree is almost always required for all types of professional library positions. Exceptions occur in special collections such as archives and museums and nonlibrary settings such as orchestras and publishers.

The position of academic music librarian, which can include any mix of management, budgeting, collection development, bibliographic instruction (BI), classroom teaching, cataloging, and computer and AV equipment support, also consistently requires an undergraduate music degree, knowledge of print and electronic music resources, communication and interpersonal skills, and commitment to public service. In addition, a graduate music degree is usually preferred, much more often than a graduate subject degree is preferred in the general academic library market. In my experience, a graduate subject degree won't just help you get a job; it will also buy you more salary. Many academic music librarian positions explicitly require experience. Some ads that don't appear to contain such a requirement at first glance actually may upon closer reading; the common phrasing is "demonstrated ability to/skills in/knowledge of." Types of required experience are often specified and may include supervision, collection development, cataloging, teaching or BI, and budgeting. Other common requirements are foreign languages (usually Western European) and active participation in national professional organizations. Conservatory music librarian positions have the same responsibilities and requirements as these, though usually with less emphasis on musicological research and more on performance.

Academic and conservatory performing arts librarian positions cover music as well as art, dance, and/or theater, and generally have the same requirements as above, with one notable difference: an expectation of familiarity with or willingness to learn about resources in the arts beyond music, and subject degrees can be in any of the arts appropriate to the position.

Academic reference librarian positions often entail music plus other arts and/or humanities and tend to require teaching, interpersonal and communication skills, and knowledge of print and electronic resources in the arts, humanities, and occasionally social sciences. A preferred graduate subject degree is less common than for music librarians, and the range of acceptable undergraduate degrees is broader, often including the humanities and sometimes the social sciences.

Academic collection development/bibliographer positions tend to exist in larger research libraries where gradute subject degrees and foreign language skills are often required. As with reference positions, the range of acceptable degrees tends to include the arts and humanities. In addition, communication and interpersonal skills are regularly required.

Academic and conservatory cataloger positions often include responsibility for music plus multimedia, humanities, and/or special collections materials. The most common requirements are knowledge of AACR2, MARC formats, Library of Congress Subject Headings (LCSH), a bibliographic network (e.g., OCLC, RLIN), automated library systems, and cataloging nonprint materials other than scores and sound recordings (e.g., AV materials, slides, electronic resources). In addition, communication and interpersonal skills, analytic and problem solving skills, foreign language skills (usually Western European), and familiarity with nontraditional cataloging standards (e.g., Dublin Core) are required. An undergraduate music degree is usually necessary, and a graduate music degree is often preferred. It is not uncommon to see project cataloging positions, which often have specialized requirements such as knowledge of Hebrew and Yiddish or familiarity with MLA's *Guidelines for Sheet Music Cataloging*.

Academic technical services positions tend to include responsibility not only for cataloging, but also for processing, mending, binding, acquisitions, and/or computer troubleshooting. Experience is usually required due to the broader and more responsible nature of the job. Ads often request experience in areas such as serials and acquisitions in addition to cataloging.

Academic technology/media positions are usually oriented toward managing media resources, although they occasionally focus on systems and information technology (IT). Media resource management positions seek knowledge of computer hardware and software, media equipment, web-based technologies, digitized sound and image management, video distribution and production, copyright issues for nonprint materials, MIDI applications, and streaming media, as well as communication and presentation skills, commitment to public service, and troubleshooting abilities. Acceptable degree areas include music, fine arts, film/video/ television, education, and instructional or media technology. Systems and IT positions seek, in addition to some of the above requirements, the ability to configure and maintain PCs, LAN servers, and related equipment, and familiarity with database design and maintenance. Educational requirements are often directed toward technology.

Academic music department librarians report to their institution's music department, not library administration. These positions may include responsibility for collection development, reference and BI, cataloging, and media and facilities management and maintenance. Educational background and experience tend to carry more weight than an ALA accredited library degree for these positions, which seek people with a music education, knowledge of media equipment, and supervisory and organizational skills.

Public library music librarian, performing arts, and reference positions usually involve music plus the fine arts and/or sports and recreation, and responsibilities often include collection development, website maintenance, and AV materials. Usual educational requirements are a library degree and an undergraduate music or fine arts degree or equivalent knowledge. Other common requirements are knowledge of AV materials, interpersonal skills—specifically tact, courtesy, patience, and flexibility—and residency within the city limits. Larger public libraries tend to require foreign language skills and experience and sometimes advertise for specialized or project-related positions.

Public library cataloger positions tend to be limited to music, sound recordings, and AV materials. A library degree and music background are the usual education requirements, and experience is rarely necessary, although public libraries typically seek familiarity with OCLC, MARC formats, AACR2, LCSH, and Dewey or LC classification.

Cataloging services such as OCLC or Follett Audiovisual Resources tend to require a library degree, desire a music background, and almost without exception require cataloging experience. Foreign language skills are sometimes also sought.

Archival positions, whether in independent archives such as the Louis Armstrong House and Archives and the Woody Guthrie Foundation and Archives or in academic institutions, vary greatly in their focus and needs because each collection is narrowly defined. In general, however, requirements include knowledge of archival practices and management, cataloging of archival materials, conservation and preservation standards, and various software applications. A media background or knowledge of audio preservation and engineering are also often sought, as are communication, interpersonal, and organizational skills. The educational requirements of independent archives tend to be a music background plus background in an area pertaining to the archive's mission, such as jazz or American folk music. Academic archives have the typical academic educational requirements, that is, library and music degrees, and often require an advanced degree in music. In all types of archives duties may include research, exhibit development, and public presentations.

Museum and archival positions often share similarities in their responsibilities and educational requirements. Museums typically seek a music background plus appropriate specialized subject knowledge, and a museum studies degree is usually acceptable in lieu of a library degree. Knowledge of various databases and software applications is typically required, and duties can include cataloging, exhibit development, educational outreach, marketing and public relations, preservation, supervising volunteers, conducting research, and helping researchers.

Orchestra librarian responsibilities can include preparation of music for rehearsal and performances, including marking bowings, serving as a resource to orchestra members and staff, managing the orchestra's music collection, correspondence and record keeping, and cataloging. Requirements vary depending on the size of the orchestra but usually include thorough knowledge of orchestral literature, a music performance background, knowledge of foreign language musical terminology, organizational and interpersonal skills, flexibility, and occasionally a library and/or music degree.

Positions with publishers and dealers vary widely in their responsibilities. Duties sought in the ads surveyed include arts administration, preparation of scores and parts for rental and retail distribution, oversight of a rental library, inventory management, making copies of out-of-print music available to customers, website maintenance, and research and cataloging of scholarly, rare and antiquarian printed music, manuscripts, and iconography. Requirements regularly include organizational and communication skills, ability to provide excellent customer service, self-motivation, and a solid background in music. Specific degree requirements are rarely stated in such ads.

Most of the government library positions advertised in the *Placement Service Job List* are from the Library of Congress. The identity of some libraries is unknown due to their seeking to fill contract positions through firms such as Library Associates and The Library Co-Op, Inc., who don't identify their clients in their ads. Government library positions are fairly evenly split between public service and cataloging responsibilities and have the same basic requirements as have been described above, that is, a library and appropriate undergraduate subject degree and experience appropriate to the level of the position. Occasionally special skills such as knowledge of braille are sought.

Positions in special libraries and organizations need to be examined individually, as each is unique in its purpose and needs. Among the special organizations that have advertised in the *Placement Service Job List* are the following:

- An unidentified library with a focus on Asian arts and humanities seeking someone to do reference, collection development, website maintenance, research, interlibrary loan, and authority work;
- The Estate Project for Artists with AIDS, seeking an arts administrator;
- RILM Abstracts, seeking editors;
- A dot-com organization seeking a researcher to provide business and legal information to the music industry;
- Jazz at Lincoln Center, seeking someone to oversee music transcription and engraving, contract negotiation, and collection development;
- RIPM, seeking a research and funding coordinator to write grant proposals, do data entry, represent RIPM at conferences, edit a bulletin, scholarly materials, and promotional materials, and coordinate RIPM's collaborators; and
- The Britten-Pears Library, seeking a librarian to develop the collection and make it available for scholarly and educational purposes.

The requirements of each of these organizations are as unique as each organization's mission. The purpose of describing these positions is not so much to help in preparation for such employment as to corroborate that a variety of unique opportunities exists under the rubric of "music library employment." Other rare opportunities posted in the *Placement Service Job List* are in school and opera libraries, so rare, in fact, as to be almost nonexistent and unnecessary to examine here.

As is evident from this overview of the music library job market as represented in MLA's *Placement Service Job List* from January 1999 through April 2003, the vast majority of music library employment opportunities exist in academic institutions, followed by public libraries and more specialized organizations. At the same time, this survey reveals that a number of nontraditional opportunities combining music and library expertise are also available to those interested in music librarianship outside a traditional library setting. An awareness of these opportunities will help those entering or moving within the music library job market

to become better equipped to direct their career interests and gain a more
thorough understanding of how to prepare themselves to follow their
chosen directions within the world of music librarianship.

Suggestions for Further Reading

Albitz, Rebecca S. "Electronic Resource Librarians in Academic
    Libraries: A Position Announcement Analysis, 1996–2001." *Portal:
    Libraries and the Academy* 2, no. 4 (October 2002): 589–600.
Beile, Penny M., and Megan M. Adams. "Other Duties as Assigned:
    Emerging Trends in the Academic Library Job Market." *College &
    Research Libraries News* 61, no. 4 (July 2000): 336–47.
Chaudhry, Abdus Sattar, and N. C. Komathi. "Requirements for
    Cataloguing Positions in the Electronic Environment." *Technical
    Services Quarterly* 19, no. 1 (2001): 1–23.
Croneis, Karen S. and Pat Henderson. "Electronic and Digital Librarian
    Positions: A Content Analysis of Announcements from 1990–2000."
    Journal of Academic Librarianship 28, no. 4 (July 2002): 232–37.
Dankner, Laura. "Job Trends, 1974–1989," in *Careers in Music
    Librarianship: Perspectives from the Field*, comp. Carol Tatian, MLA
    Technical Report,18. (Canton, MA: Music Library Association,
    1990): 43–56.
Edwards, Ronald G. "Migrating to Public Librarianship: Depart on Time
    to Ensure a Smooth Flight." *Library Trends* 5, no. 4 (Spring 2002):
    631–39.
Johnson, Timothy J. "Making It to the Major Leagues: Career Movement
    between Library and Archival Professions and from Small College
    to Large University Libraries." *Library Trends* 50, no. 4 (Spring
    2002), 614–30.
Khurshid, Zahiruddin. "The Impact of Information Technology on Job
    Requirements and Qualifications for Catalogers." *Information
    Technology and Libraries* 22, no. 1 (March 2003): 18–21.
Kwasik, Hanna. "Qualifications for a Serials Librarian in an Electronic
    Environment." *Serials Review* 28, no. 1 (Spring 2002): 33–37.
LIBJOBS: An Employment Service List for Library Professionals.
    www.ifla.org/II/lists/libjobs.htm (4 September 2003).
Lynch, Beverly P., and Kimberley Robles Smith. "The Changing Nature
    of Work in Academic Libraries." *College & Research Libraries News*
    62, no. 5 (September 2001): 407–20.

Major Orchestra Librarians' Association. Publication Committee. *The Orchestra Librarian: A Career Introduction.* 1993, rev. 2001. www.mola–inc.org/orchlib.html (4 September 2003).

Morrow, Jean. "Education for Music Librarianship." *Notes* 56, no. 3 (March 2000): 655–61.

Music Library Association. Library School Liaison Subcommittee. *Core Competencies and Music Librarians.* (April 2002) www.musiclibraryassoc.org/pdf/Core_Competencies.pdf (4 September 2003).

Music Library Association. Placement Service. *Placement Service Job List.* www.musiclibraryassoc.org/services/se_job.htm (4 September 2003).

Music OCLC Users Group Website. www.musicoclcusers.org/.

OLAC: Online Audiovisual Catalogers Website. http://ublib.buffalo.edu/libraries/units/cts/olac/ (4 September 2003).

Rodwell, John. "Dinosaur or Dynamo?: The Future for the Subject Specialist Reference Librarian." *New Library World* 10, nos. 1–2 (2001): 48–52.

White, Gary W. "Head of Reference Positions in Academic Libraries: A Survey of Job Announcements from 1990 through 1999." *Reference & User Services Quarterly* 39, no. 3 (Spring 2000): 265–72.

4

Job Hunt Rhetoric:
The Conversation behind the
Successful Search

Sheridan Stormes and Gordon Theil

The job placement process in music librarianship has several important components. Whether securing a position or securing a person to fill a position, the process in any field essentially involves these elements:

- the job posting
- the job description
- the application letter
- the résumé
- the job interview
- the job offer

How well any one of these steps is executed can have a significant impact on how effectively a position is or is not filled. In a successful search process, the importance of well-chosen language cannot be overestimated. This chapter analyzes several job postings. In addition, it presents several groups of questions that help to clarify candidates' and employers' intentions during the interview process. The combination of informative written materials and informed conversation can contribute to a positive outcome for all concerned. While these underlying principles are based on the authors' experiences in academic libraries, they are easily applicable or adaptable to public libraries as well.

Ideally, the job posting and the more detailed job description, coupled with information provided in the job application materials and the interview process, provide a means for both the library seeking an employee and the prospective applicants to make informed and appropriate decisions. To determine whether or not a particular candidate is suited to a given position (and vice versa), each party attempts to gain as much useful information about the other as possible. For the employer, the goal is to determine whether or not a candidate has the necessary abilities, experience, work ethic, and communication and interpersonal skills to be successful in the position. For the candidate, the goal is to find out whether the position offers the type of work that the candidate is seeking and, if so, whether the candidate indeed possesses the necessary expertise and experience to be successful in the job under consideration. With that in mind, the second half of this chapter will concern itself with what information should be found in well-written job postings and descriptions and with how one should appropriately (and, hopefully, successfully) respond to them.

The Job Posting

The job posting is the initial expression in a process of communication between the hiring library and the librarian candidate for a position. Job postings for academic libraries vary quite a bit, depending on the type and level of the position, the culture of the institution, and the nature of the selection process. They can be succinct and fairly basic or highly informative. Postings formally announce the position and provide the initial filtering of the candidate pool. The perusal of any two or three months' worth of postings on the Music Library Association's website job list[1] will quickly illustrate these points.

Job postings, whether extensive or brief, describe the title, basic responsibilities, and at least some of the qualifications for the position. This is the minimum that the library is seeking. Some more detailed postings may include a description of the library or parent institution and the community in which it is situated and a statement about salary and benefits. Starting date, length of appointment, an affirmative action policy statement, application procedures, and deadlines should be present as well.

Many job postings will list both "required" and "preferred" qualifications for a position. At many if not most institutions, the distinction is important. Generally speaking, no candidate who lacks any of the required qualifications for a position can (or should) be hired for a position if another candidate has all of the requirements. The more "preferred" qualifications that are listed in a posting, the more flexibility the library will have in selecting from a pool of qualified candidates the person who will fit best into the structure and culture of the organization. For instance, an organization that places a job posting listing all of the qualifications as "preferred," with the exception of a master's in library or information studies, clearly is opting for as much flexibility as possible in selection. A Syracuse University posting had a rather elegant way of handling preferred qualifications by including them as required in a paragraph that states "AND the best combination of the following."[2] Consider the following posting from the University of South Carolina for an assistant music librarian:

> The **UNIVERSITY OF SOUTH CAROLINA,** Columbia, South Carolina, is looking for an Assistant Music Librarian.
> **Description:** The USC Music Library is a branch library located in the School of Music, which has an enrollment of approximately 500 music majors. Reporting to the Head of the Music Library, the Assistant Music Librarian oversees the Music Library's special collections, including the processing of collections of manuscripts, personal papers, and other archival materials. Prepares and maintains electronic finding aids. Makes all housing and treatment decisions. Provides in-person, telephone, and e-mail reference assistance relating to the special collections. Coordinates rotating exhibits. Manages gifts-in-kind program, including decision making about appropriateness to collection, production of acknowledgments, and internal appraising. Serves as liaison with the Preservation Services department. Will train and supervise Music Library staff in basic archival procedures and oversees students working on related projects. Performs other duties as assigned. Active participation in professional activities and departmental or university initiatives. This is a full-time position (37.5 hours per week). Further information may be found at: www.sc.edu/library/music/music.html.
> **Qualifications:** *Required*: An ALA-accredited M.L.S.; a bachelor's degree in music or equivalent; formal training in archival theory and practice or equivalent experience; a thorough familiarity

with print and online music reference resources; and, excellent oral and written communication skills. *Preferred*: Graduate degree in music. Familiarity with AACR2, MARC, OCLC, and the NOTIS automated system. Strong leadership and supervisory skills. Knowledge of digital technologies. Working knowledge of at least one European language.[3]

This posting also includes a small number of required qualifications, including general statements concerning familiarity with reference resources and excellent communications skills. Almost every job posting is going to express a requirement for communication skills, which is of increasing importance as librarians are expected take on more and more cross-departmental and campuswide responsibilities. Of course, the candidate's ability to communicate will be assessed by how well the letter of application is constructed and how the candidate conducts himself or herself during the interview process.

Careful examination of the South Carolina posting strongly suggests qualified candidates for the position will have all of the required qualifications listed. Given the job responsibilities set forth, the "preferred" qualifications will play a large role in the ranking of the candidates. For example, an academic library posting a position in the current environment that includes responsibilities for special collections materials, including the creation and maintenance of electronic finding aids, will definitely be looking for someone with at least some knowledge of digital technology and its standards, even though this qualification is listed as "preferred." Possibly the requirement for "formal training in archival theory or practice or equivalent experience" also would encompass some degree of technological ability.

The phrase "or equivalent experience" brings up another point. Academic library postings vary in their requirements for graduate degrees in music. Some years ago, when there was a surplus of people applying for music library positions, job postings often required at least a second master's degree in music. While this is sometimes still the case, as with a recent Baylor University posting for a management-level music and fine arts librarian, in order to open up the pool of candidates many institutions now either only prefer a second graduate degree or require graduate work or the equivalent in the discipline. Still, generally speaking, for public service and collection development librarians in particular, most music library positions are definitely looking for strong academic music credentials along with all the other qualifications. Such credentials offer an objective standard by which the employer can initially gauge the candidate's knowledge of the discipline. Moreover, in academic institutions they help to establish credibility with faculty, which will be important in opening avenues of communication and collaboration. Most successful candidates will possess a graduate degree (or degrees) in music or significant previous academic music library experience.

On the other hand, postings for cataloging positions tend to focus more on technical and standards-based knowledge and experience and, while requiring strong knowledge of the discipline, generally do not require graduate experience. This is illustrated in the following posting for a Kent State music and media cataloging position:

> **KENT STATE UNIVERSITY** Kent, Ohio, is looking for a Music and Media Cataloger.
>
> **Description:** Kent State University Libraries and Media Services invite applications for the position of MUSIC AND MEDIA CATALOGER. The Libraries have a collection of more than 2 million volumes and hold membership in the Association of Research Libraries and the Center for Research Libraries. Kent State is a founding member of OCLC and of OhioLINK (www.library.kent.edu), Ohio's statewide information system. Innovative Interfaces is used for the integrated library system.
>
> **Responsibilities:** The successful candidate will perform original and copy cataloging of music and media, including scores and sound recordings, software, audiovisual materials, and books in all subject areas. Original cataloging copy will be contributed to OCLC. Materials to be cataloged may be housed in the Main Library collection, the Hugh A. Glauser Music Library, or any of the seven regional campus libraries. The Music and Media Cataloger will provide expertise on national and international cataloging standards, address and resolve access issues and cataloging practices for integrating electronic resources into the collection, and supervise graduate students on a variety of cataloging projects. The librarian in this position will also work closely with regional campus librarians to facilitate original and copy cataloging across an eight-campus system.
>
> **Requirements:** MLS from accredited ALA program; 2 years experience in original and complex cataloging of scores and sound recordings; experience performing original cataloging of audiovisual materials, computer files, and books; knowledge of cataloging standards, including AACR2, LC classification, LCSH, MARC21, MCD, and LCRI; academic degree in the music field.
>
> **Preferred Qualifications:** Bibliographic knowledge of one or more foreign languages; knowledge of standards for cataloging remote electronic resources.[4]

The language of the job posting also says a lot about the type of institution and the type of person it is seeking. An excellent example of this can be found in the following posting from the University of Arizona:

The **UNIVERSITY OF ARIZONA,** Tucson, Arizona, is looking for an Assistant/Associate Librarian (Music Emphasis).

Position Summary: The incumbent will work to satisfy the needs relating to instruction, research and the creative endeavors of the team's customers, particularly those in the fine arts, by matching users with appropriate resources and services. The successful candidate will contribute to the profession and the professional literature to fulfill the responsibilities of a library faculty member through service (e.g., active participation in library-related associations and organizations) and scholarship (e.g., presentations at local and national conferences and meetings, publication of original research). As member of a library profession, the Library Faculty Assembly, and the general faculty of the University, the incumbent will resist censorship of library materials and eliminate barriers to access to information, commit to intellectual freedom in the pursuit of truth and knowledge for customers and staff, commit to honesty and respect for customers and staff, commit to the professional Code of Ethics for librarianship, be involved in the governance of the Library and the University through service in the Library Faculty Assembly and on appropriate University committees, and play a leadership role on campus in ensuring that the development of information literacy is a key component of the educational experience.

Duties and Responsibilities: Fulfill primary assignment in fine arts, principally to the School of Music and Dance and related disciplines. Work in other subject areas as needed by our customers and as knowledge and ability permit. Connection Development: Establish and maintain connections with assigned group of faculty, students, researchers, and staff. May include developing programs, exhibits, and other outreach activities. Information Resources Development/Preservation: Identify, evaluate, and select information for purchase or access. Expend and manage information access funds in assigned subject areas within Information Resources Council guidelines and established allocations. Education: Develop and provide library education, course-related instruction and other specialized educational sessions to assigned customers and other groups. Develop and prepare appropriate instructional and educational aids. In-depth reference/research consultation: Develop and maintain in-depth subject knowledge of information resources and provide in-depth reference and consultations in assigned area of subject expertise. Needs Assessment: Assess and evaluate information and service needs of the teams and other customers, through application of appropriate needs assessment tools and methodologies. Undergraduate Services: Participate in and provide support for Undergraduate Services activities. These may include reference desk service, e-mail reference, instruction in general library education classes, and the training of staff and students who provide reference service. Training and Supervision: Develop and provide training sessions in areas of expertise to other team members, staff from other teams, and students in any of the above areas of responsibilities which include working closely with the Materials Access Team staff responsible for circulation, basic reference service, and physical maintenance of the Music Collection. Supervise student(s) in support activities as needed. Library-wide Responsibilities: Participate in library strategic projects teams, cross-functional teams and other teams as needed to complete the goals of the library.

Minimum Qualifications: Master's degree in Library/ Information Science from an ALA-accredited institution.

Preferred Qualifications: Graduate level course work in Music. At least four years of experience as a Music Librarian in an academic library. Experience in music cataloging. Reading knowledge of German, French, Italian, or Spanish. Ability and desire to work in a team-based environment. Evidence or knowledge of collection development and preservation, instruction, knowledge management, advanced mediated services, and needs assessment in the fine arts. Strong commitment to information access in alternative and traditional formats. Demonstrated proficiency with related electronic technology. Ability to teach in a classroom, computer lab, in a collaborative setting, or one-on-one situations. Ability to communicate and to work effectively with faculty, customers and colleagues. Demonstrated commitment to continuous learning and professional development. Demonstrated contribution to the profession through scholarship and service activities. Commitment to diversity in the academic environment. Ability to set and achieve performance goals. Knowledge of instructional techniques and methods. Knowledge of digital imaging and electronic applications in the fine arts.[5]

This description includes terms such as "team" and "leadership role," attended by language describing shared processes and administration. The expression clearly suggests that the library is looking for someone who is willing and capable of taking personal responsibility in a highly collaborative team environment; someone who is likely to be a self-starter, nonhierarchical, and with good interpersonal skills; someone who is interested in working in an administrative and organizational structure that is different from that of the traditional academic library.

Postings like Arizona's, which contain terms such as "customers," "information literacy," and "needs assessment," also suggest a significant organizational emphasis on direct and proactive user service, with an emphasis on library instruction that goes well beyond the individual discipline. In such positions, one can expect involvement in developing and implementing usability studies, focus groups, surveys, and other such approaches to customer service. The phrases "play a leadership role on campus" with regard to information literacy and "work in other subject areas as needed by our customers" suggest, as do other parts of this posting, that the incumbent in this position will be expected to have a scope of activity and responsibility that goes beyond the discipline of music.

The Job Description

Although the candidate will apply for a given position in response to a job posting only, additional details of the job should be included in the position's full job description. Often an applicant will receive a copy of the full job description if and when he or she is invited for an interview. If not, certainly it is permissible to request one at that point. Sometimes the job description is presented at the interview itself. A well-written job description will contain the following information:

- the position title (as it appears in the organizational chart, personnel records, and employment advertising), the name of the library and/or institution, a brief (often one sentence) statement of the basic job function, the position's minimum qualifications (education and skill requirements as well as personal qualifications);
- the position's supervisor, the names of the positions to whom the position gives supervision, the names of other departments that interact with the position;
- a list of the major responsibilities of the position including a description of the position's authority (e.g., decision-making limitations, budgetary limitations, etc.); and

- a statement of standards of performance against which the person holding the position will be evaluated.

Though the job description should contain information about each of these areas, by necessity such information will be brief. Most job descriptions are no more than one to three pages in length. Therefore, the main points of the job description should serve as an outline on which the candidate may base additional questions during the course of the interview.

The Application Letter

Once a candidate's interest in a position has been piqued by a particular posting, he or she will probably want to browse the website of the library/ institution that posted the job to get some idea of its culture and structure. If the candidate still finds the position attractive, he or she should put together and promptly send the appropriate application materials. Just as there is much information that a candidate will want to ascertain about a position before applying for it, there are specific things that most employers look for in a candidate's application before making a decision to extend an invitation to an interview. The first impression an employer receives about a candidate comes through the candidate's application letter and résumé. At the very least, the letter should be neat and legible and should be free of grammatical and/or spelling errors. When it comes to reviewing these letters, attention to such detail often can make or break a candidate's chances of being asked for an interview.

The letter should state as specifically as possible what attracted the candidate to the position. It should address most if not all points relating to qualifications and experience in the job posting and attempt to document possession of the required skills. This tells the employer why a particular candidate is worthy of serious consideration for the position. Simply saying that one is applying for "x" position in response to the ad seen in "x" publication and enclosing a résumé is most definitely not enough! Many times a search committee must review dozens of applications for a position. It's a tedious process. Many applicants may have résumés that indicate all the required qualifications. In reading a cover letter, the supervisor or search committee member wants to know what makes a particular applicant more worthy of serious consideration for the job than the others.

The successful applicant will clearly and succinctly articulate this information in the letter of application. Generally, the only applicants most employers are willing to consider for an interview are those who respond directly and effectively to the posting. To effectively respond to the requirements of a position, one does not necessarily need to show the exact previous job experience or qualifications described in the posting. An applicant may well have other personal and work experience that bears on the job qualifications. For example, digital recording experience gained from work on personal projects may translate to potential in support of library digital audio service; retail experience may support a strong public or "customer" service orientation; or substantial experience with national standards in one area may exemplify one's ability to learn and implement standards in a different area. What matters is that the applicant demonstrates how his or her experiences and education pertain to the job as described and that the applicant respond in some manner to as many of the job requirements listed as possible. It is helpful, too, for the candidate to give some indication of what aspect or aspects of the position specifically motivated him or her to apply for it.

The Résumé

The design and content of a résumé also can significantly affect an applicant's chances for securing an interview. Once again, the document should be neat, legible, typed, and free of grammatical and spelling errors. It should state clearly somewhere near the top of the first page the candidate's name, address, telephone number, and e-mail address (if applicable). A succinct statement of one's career objective is appropriate as well. The career objective should be neither too narrow nor too broad and should be tied in some way to the specific job for which the candidate is applying. The résumé should include the applicant's educational history in chronological order (preferably with dates) and include the full name and location of the educational institutions attended, the names of degrees and dates degrees were conferred, the academic major (for nonlibrary degrees), and other areas of concentration. It is perfectly permissible (and often highly advisable) to include grade point averages, honors, and awards. The résumé also should include a work history in reverse chronological order with dates and a brief description of the work performed. (If the applicant prefers not to give specific dates, she or he should indicate the number of months or years worked in each job.) It is generally best not to include personal information, such as age, ethnic group, health, hobbies, marital status, religion, or sex.[6]

Apart from the specific discipline-related and professional requirements of a position, most employers seek candidates with certain personal qualities and skills. These qualities and skills (or lack thereof) frequently are observable through the manner in which a candidate conducts himself or herself throughout the course of the interview process. For more definite confirmation and additional information, most prospective employers will want to contact references for the candidates about which they are the most serious. The candidate can facilitate this by appending the names, titles, addresses, and phone numbers of at least three references to the end of his or her résumé. If possible, it is best to include the name of one's current supervisor as one of the references. Special circumstances may prompt some candidates to request that their current supervisor not be contacted. Candidates should be aware that such a request can raise a red flag in the minds of those reviewing the application. Therefore, it is advisable to provide some explanation for such a request in the application materials or during the course of the interview. Whether the candidate chooses to include a letter of recommendation in the application materials or is asked to solicit a letter to be sent directly to the hiring institution, such a letter will be most valuable if it addresses the following:

- the writer's relationship to the applicant
- how long and in what capacity the writer has known the applicant
- the applicant's special strengths, skills, and areas that may need development
- an assessment of the applicant's interpersonal skills
- a recommendation about the types of jobs for which the candidate is best suited[7]

To be useful to the prospective employer, a letter of recommendation should offer a balanced assessment of the candidate's abilities, not simply a list of his or her best qualities.

The Interview

Once a candidate has been called for an interview, he or she should research the library and its parent institution and/or the community in which it is situated. This can be accomplished in a variety of ways, the simplest of which may be to visit the library's website. Most library websites contain plenty of information about the structure and culture of the hiring institution and often include the position titles of the library's professional and support staff members, a breakdown of administrative teams (if such teams exist), and mission and vision statements. If desired, additional information can be obtained by requesting information from the library's personnel office, and/or by contacting colleagues. One should come to the interview with sufficient relevant background information to indicate to those conducting the interview that one indeed is serious about the position. During the interview, the candidate should seek to obtain additional information that will be useful in making a decision about whether or not to accept the position if it is offered. This can be accomplished by simply asking tactful questions. Of course, there may always be some information that is not available or that will require conjecture on the part of the applicant.

Another area the candidate might want to explore during the course of the interview is the organizational structure of the library and the unit or branch:

- How layered is the hierarchy, and who reports to whom?
- Where does the position's supervisor stand in the structure, and to whom does she or he report?
- How many levels separate the position's supervisor from the head of the library? This could be indicative of the potential effectiveness of the supervisor as an advocate.
- What positions in the library would be considered peer positions?
- To what extent would the successful candidate be expected or encouraged to participate in library functions outside of the position's designated unit?

The level of autonomy of the music library or music collection might be an area for serious consideration and discussion during the interview as well:

- Would the person hired to fill the position be working in a full-service unit separated from the main library (i.e., a branch library or separate floor of the main library that provides for its own ordering and receiving, cataloging, reference, reserve, interlibrary loan, and circulation services)?
- Or would the person be working in a section of the main library with a specific service designation, such as "public services," "technical services," "special collections," etc.?
- Where are the various components of the music collection (such as books, scores, recordings, videos, etc.) housed?
- Under whose jurisdiction are the listening facilities and maintenance of media equipment?
- Who is responsible for course reserves in the music or performing arts area? Are the performing scores housed in the library or the music building (if they are separate physical entities)?
- Who has control of and where are the scores housed for the school's larger performing ensembles (i.e., the band, orchestra, and choral music collections)?
- What additional responsibilities might the candidate expect to have within the library or parent organization that are not specifically listed in the posting (e.g., covering the circulation desk as necessary, providing backup support for other library units)?

A candidate also might raise questions about the committee structure of the library:

- How many and what types of committees/teams exist to support governance of and planning for the library?
- Do they seem to be standing committees, ad hoc, or a mix? If the candidate can see a list of committee memberships, he or she should note the representation on the committees—are all of the library constituencies represented in some way?
- Are the same people on many committees, or is there a generous mix of different people serving on them?
- How might the successful candidate be involved in these committees, and to what extent might he or she be expected to be involved generally with library-wide planning and governance?

- Is committee participation a condition of merit increase or
  promotion?

The culture of the library as a whole is worthy of investigation. In
the course of the interview day, does the candidate get a sense of
collegiality and collaboration among all the staff or a sense of a more
sectionalized, maybe even balkanized, situation? The involvement of
staff in the interview process can be a good indicator. The candidate
should also try to get a sense of how his or her own expectations and
proclivities fit into the existing library culture. The quality and quantity
of communication in a given work environment can play a significant
role in determining whether or not that environment is desirable or
acceptable. During the course of the interview, the candidate may wish
to ask questions to determine the following:

- What is the relationship between the professional and support
  staff or between managers and nonmanagers within the library
  and the unit? The functional distinctions between librarians
  and nonlibrarians are not always as clearly defined as they
  used to be, and more significant distinctions are now often
  based on functional hierarchies.
- Is there a defined, vertically classed society within the unit
  the candidate is investigating, or does the unit have a flatter,
  more horizontal structure?
- Does the administration solicit input from the staff in the
  decision-making process?
- How and to what degree is information disseminated among
  the various units of the library?
- Does there seem to be a healthy flow of communication from
  the staff to the administration and vice versa?
- Strong, positive relationships with faculty constituencies are
  often crucial to the success of music and arts librarians.
  Therefore, it is important to determine during the course of
  the interview the nature of the relationship between the library
  and the departments it serves. A good indication of this is the
  presence (or absence) of faculty members in the interview
  process.
- Are there any faculty members on the search committee?

- Are faculty given some opportunity or, perhaps, a specific time to meet with the candidates as part of the interview?

Additional Considerations

Finally, the candidate will want to gain as much information as possible about the standards against which the performance of the person filling the position will be evaluated. Ironically, a "standards of performance" statement, while in many ways one of the most critical aspects of a job, is frequently absent from the job description. If the performance expectations of a position are not spelled out, the applicant should inquire about them during the interview. Hopefully, this can be accomplished when the candidate meets with the position's supervisor, unit head, or the library's human resources director. In fact, it might be advantageous to bring up questions about performance expectations in more than one meeting of the interview. If responses from the various constituencies don't match, it may signal an undesirable work situation. Questions that ask about frequency, degree of accuracy, and quantity in relation to specific responsibilities should help to establish in both the mind of the employer and the mind of the applicant what the standard performance levels are for a given position.

Beyond daily job performance, one of the trickiest areas to interpret relates to professional involvement and/or creativity and research expectations. Regarding professional matters, it is useful to know the status of librarians on the campus:

- Are they faculty, staff, academic?
- How they are reviewed for merit increase and/or promotion?
- Are the librarians unionized or otherwise professionally organized?
- What will be the expectations of the library and the supervisor in terms of participation in professional activities outside the position's direct job responsibilities?

Job postings provide varying amounts of information about this. If specific statements about involvement in professional activities such as those found in the Arizona and South Carolina postings are absent, the candidate definitely will want to learn more about this. Probably the best way is to ask the human resources officer for the library, with whom the candidate should have an opportunity to meet at some point during the interview. When meeting with a unit head, the candidate should try to learn that individual's personal expectations for the position and vision for the unit. This meeting also provides an excellent opportunity to obtain some historical and situational context for the position, and it gives the candidate a chance to ask questions relating to professional goals and job-related concerns. Also, during the interview candidates for an academic library position should bear in mind the importance of demonstrating the self-assurance necessary to work assertively and actively with faculty, graduate students, and professional colleagues. In most cases, the candidate who possesses a strong knowledge of the profession and the subject discipline, along with a strong service orientation, will exude such self-assurance naturally. In any event, while a candidate should never attempt to inflate his or her abilities or experience, he or she should be careful not to downplay the skills and experience that he or she does possess.

In addition, academic library search committees will likely seek candidates who welcome involvement in library-wide (or university-wide) committee work and programs. Candidates for such positions should be desirous of such involvement and seek an opportunity to express that desire to the search committee members. Evidence of familiarity with applicable standards, initiatives, and formats relating to the particular responsibilities listed in the posting is also something that employers look for in applications and interviews. For example, in a candidate for a digital projects librarian, it would be reasonable to expect familiarity with Encoded Archival Description, Dublin Core, and the Open Archives Initiative. In fact, in the current environment, for any library-related position, one would generally expect candidates to display not only a strong comfort level with computers but also an attitude that favors the creative use of technology. Many libraries today enjoy a collaborative decision-making environment. This prompts prospective employers and search committee members to look for colleagues who will be willing and able to help reshape the vision of the library and plan strategically rather than simply perform tasks and responsibilities routinely and provide services as assigned. Candidates should bear this in mind when they are answering questions and/or given opportunities to ask questions during an interview. In preparing for an interview, candidates should thoughtfully consider not only the role of the particular position for which they are applying and how it relates to the parent institution but also the current and future role of libraries in their particular community and in society as a whole. In general, the ability to mentally step outside the boundaries of one's small sphere of influence and see the "big picture" is highly valued.

The Job Offer

Perhaps the single and most important question that an employer must ask before offering a position to any candidate is, "What is the likelihood that this person will be successful in this position?" Job searches are costly to organizations. They involve a great investment of time and resources. A heavy turnover rate among their employees is expensive and undesirable. Therefore, employers want to select the candidate who is not only the most qualified for the position but also who exhibits the greatest interest in the position and the organization with which it is affiliated. They want to select someone who will be a good colleague, getting along with and cooperating with fellow workers, and, ideally, someone who will be happy with the work and, if applicable, the living environment.

The hunting and hiring process is a two-way communication. The employer must create a carefully constructed job posting and job description and conduct a responsible review of applications. The prospective employee must scrutinize the job posting and job description, present application materials that specifically address the requirements of the job, and select references that can and will give an overall positive but also honest and balanced view of the candidate's qualifications. During the interview, a candidate's informed, enthusiastic, and confident demeanor will make a positive impression on the prospective employer. In return, a prospective employer's thoughtful attention to the candidate's responses and miscellaneous questions will make a similar impression. Together, these factors can go a long way to ensure the success of both the candidate and the search.

Suggestions for Further Reading

Broadway, Rita. "Job Descriptions Vis-à-Vis Job Applications: A Match Often Not Made in Heaven." Workshop report from the 1991 NASIG Conference. *The Serials Librarian* 21, nos. 2–3 (1991): 197–200.

DeLon, Barbara A. "Job Descriptions: What They Are, Are Not, and Can Be." *College & Research Libraries News* 6 (June 1994): 339–40.

"Guts, Brains, and Sensitivity or the Ability to Stoop, Lift, and Reach to High Places—What Makes a Good Librarian?" *Library Personnel News* 6, no. 6 (November-December 1992): 4+.

Writing Library Job Descriptions. Topics in Personnel, no. 7. Chicago: American Library Association. Office for Library Personnel Resources, 1985.

Notes

1. Music Library Association, Placement Service, *MLA Job List,* http://musiclibraryassoc.org (25 June 2003).

2. *MLA Job List,* November 2002, www.musiclibraryassoc.org/services/se_nov02.html (25 June 2003,

3. *MLA Job List,* October 2002, www.musiclibraryassoc.org/services/se_oct02.html (25 June 2003).

4. *MLA Job List,* November 2002.

5. *MLA Job List,* November 2002.

6. Rita Broadway, "Job Descriptions Vis-à-Vis Job Applications: A Match Often Not Made in Heaven," Workshop report from the 1991 NASIG Conference. *The Serials Librarian* 21, nos. 2–3 (1991): 197–200.

7. Broadway, "Job Descriptions."

5

Mid-Career Job Satisfaction: Plateaus and Passages

Linda W. Blair

Librarians of all types, academic or public, specialist or generalist, are overall quite satisfied with their chosen profession, as a number of research studies have demonstrated. One study found the turnover rate for full-time public librarians to be low compared to other occupational categories and that this low rate of turnover held true no matter what the size of the library studied.[1] A survey of long-term academic librarians in Canada found high levels of career commitment, reflected in both survey answers and written comments, and that satisfaction with the profession in general seemed to outweigh any negative factors associated with the particular organization in which they worked.[2] Arvid J. Bloom and Christina W. McCawley grouped members of a Pennsylvania library association into the categories of director, specialist, and supervisor, a category that overlapped somewhat with specialist. They found that across all categories, 61 percent reported being satisfied with their jobs, with specialists, a category that would certainly include music librarians of any sort, reporting the highest level of satisfaction of all, at 69 percent.[3] And in fact, the report of the Music Library Association Working Group Surveying Music Library Personnel Characteristics found that 82 percent of respondents were satisfied with their current jobs, and 84 percent were satisfied with the profession in general.[4]

What is it in particular that librarians like about their jobs? Among other things, a large majority of librarians in Bloom and McCawley's study reported that their jobs "tapped a good variety of their skills," and many reported appreciation for the freedom from close supervision they enjoyed. Eighty-eight percent agreed that they had the responsibility for deciding how their jobs get done.[5] A survey of academic librarians in a Southeastern library association reported that what they most appreciated about their jobs was the value of their service.[6] And similarly, a national survey of Canadian university librarians found that the most satisfying aspect of their work was their relationship to the library's users, and that surprisingly this held true even for librarians in positions with little user contact, such as catalogers and systems librarians.[7]

Another somewhat surprising research finding is that many librarians stay within the profession for their entire working lives, in contrast to those in most other occupational groups, who generally experience multiple careers over the course of their lifetime.[8] Leckie and Brett found that more than 62 percent of the librarians surveyed in their study had more than 15 years' experience as librarians.[9]

What Keeps Music Librarians in the Music?

Do the findings of research conducted across general populations of librarians hold true for music librarians? Inspired by the title of Lanier's research study "What Keeps Academic Librarians in the Books?" I asked several longtime music librarians to share their thoughts on what has kept them interested and involved over the course of a long career. No one quoted in this chapter has less than 15 years' experience in the profession and most have a good deal more.

Ralph Papakhian is head of Technical Services in the William and Gayle Cook Music Library, Indiana University. In Ralph's view, the music itself is at the heart of what keeps him vitally interested in the profession.

> My primary interest in music librarianship has been and is the materials of music. I suppose this interest developed during high school, when I spent many Saturdays roaming around the shelves of the Detroit Public Library Music and Drama Department. The stuff of music was intriguing. In library school I found cataloging to be the area that kept me in touch with that stuff (as well as being the most intellectually challenging course).
>
> Fortunately, I was hired as a music cataloger at the Indiana University Music Library—a library where there is plenty of musical stuff. The fascination continues. All artistic endeavors, including

music, are based on the discovery or creation of something new. The stuff of music, whether new music newly published, or old music newly published, or old music newly acquired or found, is a constant stream of change. At least from my perspective, I have not felt a need to change my work since I still am excited by the materials of music, the handling of those materials, and as a cataloger, the description and arrangement of those materials.

I would also say that my job has additional components that help to stimulate that interest in music materials. I do have the opportunity to teach staff, student assistants, and music librarianship student interns about cataloging. This teaching component provides a social context in which to work with music publications. There is sort of a collective joy at encountering new and interesting problems to solve. I must also mention the fact that the Indiana University School of Music is driven by a quest for excellence in all aspects of musical performance and scholarship. Working in such an environment is certainly stimulating. The school also provides a venue for almost constant live performance of music. Hearing live music performed intelligently and enthusiastically is exhilarating and informs my work as a music cataloger.[10]

Linda Solow Blotner, head of the Allen Library, University of Hartford, which houses music, theater, and dance materials, contributed the following thoughts on her career:

For me, remaining in music librarianship has been about the music. I've always wanted to be around music—the music itself in its various formats and the people professionally connected to it. I enjoyed the atmosphere of academic libraries too, but it was not until I discovered music libraries that I knew just what I wanted to do with my future. This profession seemed to combine everything I was interested in— music, education, the academic environment, and people—with my own particular set of abilities and talents.

I was particularly lucky because my career discovery happened when I was a student at Brooklyn College at the time that Walter Gerboth was both music librarian and president of MLA. It was the greatest introduction to the profession one could have! Walter involved me in many special projects when I was an undergraduate student, and working with him on these made me want to stay on at Brooklyn for a masters in music. He was so full of energy, so enthusiastic, smart, and challenging that music librarianship became for me a clear goal. One of the significant things I learned from him that has been with me for my entire career was the breadth of activities a music librarian has available—I couldn't imagine ever being bored because of the variety of people and projects that I have always found waiting around the next corner.

I think academic music librarians have a special relationship with their faculty that most other librarians—even subject specialists—do not enjoy with other faculty. I've assumed that this mutual affinity was due to the music training that music librarians share with their faculty so that they all see themselves as part of the same family on campus. And the music students are part of this too. Since music is a vocation and avocation, there is a lot of room for professional and social overlap.

Over the years opportunities have arisen to move into an administrative position, or out of a library, but I've never opted to pursue them because I have very much enjoyed middle-management positions that combine hands-on access to materials and people with enough managerial responsibilities to believe that I can influence decisions and outcomes in support of educational music programs. It's been a good balance for me.

MLA has been the perfect means of bringing all of these themes together for me.[11]

Several commonplaces occur in these two narratives, and they can be summarized as (1) the environment, (2) the people, and (3) the music. For many music librarians, the presence of these attributes, and their interaction, creates a balance that sustains interest and motivation throughout many years in the same career and indeed, even in the same position.

The Environment

Librarians of all kinds are often heard to say they fell in love with libraries during their youth or student years. And some individuals who enjoyed their student years more than the "real world" may find their niche as librarians. One can be a professional student in the best sense, by actually being paid for it. And as for work settings, most libraries are lovely places—generally orderly, sometimes physically magnificent, and almost always quiet, although to say so may bring to mind some unwelcome stereotypes. This is not to say that work in libraries is never hectic or stressful, but there is general agreement that compared to many other work environments, libraries have advantages both in physical attractiveness and in inherent associations. Libraries embody education, the exchange of ideas, the preservation of the products of human creativity and endeavor, and a sense of history and continuity. Yet at the same time, libraries are dynamic, constantly growing and changing. Many music librarians enjoy the dynamic interplay of ideas and objects that surrounds them daily. The continuity in library practice that allows for scores published a century apart to reside next to one another on the shelf, coupled with the ongoing march of new technologies and new materials, results in a satisfying mix, providing a sense of integration and balance. These are among the intangible benefits of a career in librarianship.

The People

Music librarians, almost always musicians themselves of one sort or another, enjoy a sense of common experience, knowledge, and culture with the people they meet in the course of their work on a daily basis. These associations include not only community library users, students, and faculty, but also other music librarians with whom they interact at work and in the activities of professional associations such as the Music Library Association, the Association for Recorded Sound Collections, and the International Association of Music Libraries. Compared to other professions, the music library profession is relatively small and a large percentage of its practitioners know one another. This is often cited as one of the most rewarding aspects of the career.

Like Linda Solow Blotner, many music librarians speak of mentors who inspired them or encouraged them to enter the profession. Later in their careers, these same librarians enjoy the rewards of working with like-minded younger or new-to-the-profession colleagues as they step into the roles of mentors and teachers themselves, helping to guide promising individuals into the field. It is impossible to predict the future of any profession with certainty, because complex interactions of economic and demographic trends affect them, but there are indications that a shortage of librarians, especially in the academic field, may be on the horizon.[12] Mentoring and recruitment serve to maintain the health of the profession as a whole, while providing opportunities for mid–career librarians to remain vital in their own professions.

The Music

The most pervasive theme running through the narratives above is that of music itself. Many music librarians cite the importance of lifelong involvement with music as the single most important factor in their ongoing job satisfaction. For music librarians, this intellectual engagement with the subject matter and contact with the materials and products of the discipline are powerful motivators to join and remain in the profession.

Most music librarians are individuals with a strong background in music and strong desire to remain involved with music who also have talents for organization, teaching, management, or technology. Music librarianship provides the opportunity to use these diverse talents together with immersion in a stimulating musical community, as well as access to a seemingly infinite array of musical scores, recordings, videos, and printed material about music—all this and exceptional borrowing privileges to go with it.

Plateaus and Strategies to Avoid Them

While some music librarians find the challenges and rewards inherent in their positions satisfying over the course of many years, others may need to seek change for various reasons. Some may feel the need for advancement and will find it in higher-level positions within music librarianship or outside of it. Others may feel the need for change but for various reasons, such as family concerns or geographic limitations, may find it difficult to move into a different position. In "Midlife Career Decisions of Librarians," a 2002 special issue of *Library Trends,* Denise L. Montgomery cites J. M. Bardwick, providing definitions for several types of plateauing.[13] One type of plateauing, content plateauing, may occur when an individual has mastered what there is to know in his or her current position and may begin to feel there is nothing new left to learn. But more commonly the type of plateauing referred to in the literature is structural plateauing, which occurs "when an employee reaches the highest level he or she can go in the company."[14] Montgomery does note that librarians are probably less prone to dissatisfaction with structural plateauing than those working in other professions because their organizations are generally smaller, with fewer levels of administration and in general because most librarians are not drawn to the work by the possibility of wielding power. [15]

Nevertheless, there are bound to be situations where music librarians may feel they have plateaued, and both management and individuals within the profession need to be aware of ways to make these individuals feel rewarded, not only for their continued professional development, but also to ensure that the organization retains valuable, experienced librarians. The next section explores some of the possible solutions to prevent or relieve career plateauing should it occur.

Leaves of Absence

In another article from "Midlife Career Decisions of Librarians," Marlis Hubbard explores some options for sabbatical leaves, such as internships, job exchanges, conference participation, community service, travel, and of course, study and research. She concludes, "Creating sabbaticals that are truly invigorating is not only possible but also crucial to one's well being."[16] Even in organizations where true sabbatical leaves are not part of the contract, it is often possible to negotiate leaves of various types, ranging in length from one or two weeks to several months. The MLA Personnel Subcommittee offered a several-year series of programs at the annual MLA meeting on topics of international job exchanges, internships, and various types of sabbatical leaves. In all of these sessions, MLA members spoke about their successful ventures at home and abroad in finding opportunities for study and exchange that enriched their careers and their lives, proving that such endeavors are as possible for music librarians as they are for generalists.

Flexibility

Library work lends itself to flexible schedules of various kinds, and this flexibility can be a very attractive aspect for individuals at any phase of their careers. Technical services jobs are especially amenable to flexible schedules, but there is often room for compromise in other types of jobs as well. Because libraries are often open evenings and weekends, some positions allow for nonstandard schedules that may sometimes be tailored to individual needs.

Institutions are becoming more aware of the value of offering flexible schedules as mutually beneficial for both employees and the organizations they serve. The University of Rochester has enacted the following policy concerning flexible scheduling:

> The University encourages departments whenever practicable to provide flexibility in work schedules for staff who are unable to work regular full-time or regular part-time hours throughout the year. By providing flexibility in scheduling, the University may be able to retain valued employees and maximize savings.[17]

Among the types of schedules available under this policy are reduced appointments (less than twelve months), job shares, and part-time work. Such flexible schedules can be invaluable to librarians who are balancing work and family priorities while they are caring for young children, and again later in their careers when they may be caring for aging parents. They may also provide niches of time for research and writing in positions where sabbatical leaves are not possible. And they can be very attractive to musicians who want to combine their library career with continued involvement in performance or teaching.

Restructuring

As Montgomery states, in cases where there are "more good people in the organization than there are positions to which they can be promoted, . . . restructuring the organization to eliminate levels of management or instituting team-based management can work very well as solutions to the problem of structural plateauing."[18] Besides those listed by Montgomery, restructuring can take other forms and can still work to invigorate careers. For example, a cataloger may take on some duties in reference and bibliographic instruction to become more connected to the user community. Or a public services librarian may take on some duties in cataloging, providing an opportunity to learn new skills and to become more aware of the principles underlying the online catalog.

Jennifer Bowen is head of Technical Services at the Sibley Music Library, Eastman School of Music, and head of cataloging for the University of Rochester. She describes the restructuring that provided the opportunity for her to move into a higher level position in cataloging and technical services management, making use of her knowledge and leadership skills while still remaining involved in music librarianship:

Fifteen years ago I started work at the Sibley Music Library as a music cataloger, then over the years progressed to Head of Technical Services. During these years I also became involved in university-wide library activities, such as implementing our new online system and outsourcing authority control. Being involved in broader projects like this enabled me to develop a perspective that looked beyond seeing only the needs of the music library, and people noticed that. I started being asked to coordinate some of these projects, and I found that I had created a reputation for myself within the University of Rochester libraries as someone who could get things done. In 2000 I was offered a position as head of Cataloging for the entire university in addition to keeping my position at Sibley. It is the perfect job for me right now in that it has enabled me to still keep my hand in the music world while also engaging in new areas that I never would have been exposed to had I stayed solely at the Sibley Library. The key to this was in my creating working relationships with colleagues outside of the music library. When the other libraries had a need to fill, the administration was willing to find a way around the institutional bureaucracy to create this unique dual position for me.[19]

Personal Strategies

Management must do whatever is possible to motivate and retain valuable mid–career librarians, but it is always a wise course of action for individuals to take steps to direct their own career development as well. Geraldine Laudati, a music librarian for approximately twenty-seven years, spent thirteen years at the University of Wisconsin-Madison as director of the Mills Music Library. At the 2002 meeting of the Music Library Association in Las Vegas, she spoke at the Personnel Subcommittee open session on strategies for maintaining vitality in one's career. She has provided the following paraphrase of her remarks, all of which focus on strategies that individual librarians can employ to take responsibility for their own continuing development:

1. Commit to lifelong learning: make it a personal goal to learn something new each year, or as often as your comfort level permits. Take a course, hire a trainer, whatever it takes. Oh, and make sure it's something you want to know about.

2. Look for partnerships and collaborations. Language, folklore, communications, business, or area studies departments offer wonderful opportunities to pursue grants, host conferences, etc.,

bringing the Music Library to the spotlight and affording
opportunities to learn something new, meet new colleagues, and
bring new clientele to library. Along the same lines, collaborate
with other library departments on projects whenever possible.

3. Get involved in teaching: working with students and mentoring
    keeps us up to date with what's happening and helps keep us
    young. Look for opportunities in the School of Music,
    Information Literacy programs, or library school, if possible.

4. Schedule job hunts, perhaps in areas outside your own, but
    always for positions that carry more responsibility than the one
    you are in. This forces the issue of keeping current in many
    areas.

5. Make yourself available for temporary administrative duties
    outside the Music Library. I find that doing two jobs often helps
    me better perform in my position because it forces me to be
    more efficient and to spend less time on tasks that really should
    be done by someone else.

6. Engage in new technologies. While very occasionally, the
    appearance of yet another program change to my desktop makes
    me want to scream, exploring the remarkable opportunities
    afforded to music by new and emerging technologies is a
    constant growth experience. It doesn't even have to be difficult—
    electronic selection for example has made a dent in the incredible
    paper flow of selection tools.

7. Be creative and flexible. Apply the same resourcefulness we've
    had to use to promote our music libraries all along to personal
    and career growth.

8. Have fun. This sounds absurd but in the cosmic scheme of things,
    work consumes the majority of our lives. Finding something to
    enjoy and making work fun for your staff and even for your
    clientele cannot help but to bring vitality to a unit. I think this is
    an acquired attitude.[20]

So in the end, what does keep music librarians on the job over the
long term? Like the librarians surveyed in the studies above, they
appreciate their autonomy, they share a dedication to service and they
feel that their jobs draw on a good variety of their skills. They also enjoy
working in an academic or educational setting. But to many who have

chosen a specialization in music librarianship, it is the lifelong involvement with music and musicians that remains paramount. It is the *sine qua non*—the reason they come, *and* the reason they stay.

Notes

1. Richard Rubin, "Employee Turnover Among Full-Time Public Librarians," *Library Quarterly,* 59, no. 1 (1999): 27–46.

2. Donna M. Millard, "Why Do We Stay? Survey of Long-Term Academic Librarians in Canada," *Portal: Libraries and the Academy,* 3, no. 1 (2003): 109.

3. Arvid J. Bloom and Christina W. McCawley, "Job Satisfaction in the Library Profession: Results and Implications from a Pennsylvania Survey," *Library Administration & Management,* 7, no. 2 (Spring 1993): 91.

4. David Lesniaski, "Profile of the Music Library Association Membership: Report of the Working Group Surveying Music Library Personnel Characteristics," *Notes* 56, no. 4 (June 2000): 901.

5. Bloom and McCawley, "Job Satisfaction," 92–93.

6. Patricia Lanier et al., "What Keeps Academic Librarians in the Books?" *The Journal of Academic Librarianship* 23, no. 3 (May 1997): 193.

7. Gloria J. Leckie and Jim Brett, "Job Satisfaction of Canadian University Librarians: A National Survey," *College & Research Libraries* 58, no. 1 (January 1997): 36.

8. Leckie and Brett, "Job Satisfaction," 31.

9. Leckie and Brett, "Job Satisfaction," 35.

10. Ralph Papakhian, personal correspondence, July 2003.

11. Linda Solow Blotner, personal correspondence, July 2003.

12. See, for example, Rebecca T. Lenzini, "The Graying of the Library Profession: A Survey of Our Professional Association and Their Responses," *Searcher* 10, no. 7 (August 2002): 88–97; and Stanley Wilder, "The Changing Profile of Research Library Professional Staff," *ARL Monthly Report* 208/209, www.arl.org/newsltr/208_209/chgprofile.htm (20 July 2003).

13. Daniel F. Phelan and Richard M. Malinski, eds. Midlife Career Decisions of Librarians. *Library Trends* 50, no. 4 (Spring 2002).

14. J. M. Bardwick, *The Plateauing Trap: How to Avoid it in Your Career—and Your Life* (New York: American Management Association, 1986), cited in Denise L. Montgomery, "Happily Ever After: Plateauing as a Means for Long-Term Career Satisfaction,"*Library Trends* 50, no. 4 (Spring 2002).

15. Denise L. Montgomery, "Happily Ever After.

16. Marlis Hubbard, "Exploring the Sabbatical or Other Leave as a Means of Energizing a Career," *Library Trends* 50, no. 4 (Spring 2002): 603–13.

6

The Game Remains the Same: Moving between Academic and Public Libraries

Jeanette L. Casey

Music librarians like their jobs. According to the 1997 Profile of MLA members,[1] more than 82 percent are satisfied or highly satisfied with their current job. This percentage goes up even higher, to 84 percent, when measuring satisfaction with our profession in general. Add this to the relatively small number of music library positions available, and it isn't surprising to hear of music librarians keeping the same job throughout their careers. When desirous of a change, what's a mid-career music librarian to do? Moving up within the same institution often means becoming a general administrator. Moving up and out to a head music librarian position at a larger institution is a rare opportunity and generally requires geographic relocation. Moving laterally to a similar institution sometimes hardly seems worth the upheaval.

There is another possibility: a lateral move to a *different type* of institution. This allows one to remain a music librarian, yet provides plenty of new and interesting challenges and may not even require relocation. This type of career move was the topic of a panel discussion, "Crossing the Great Divide," sponsored by the Public Libraries Committee at MLA's 2003 Annual Meeting. Vic Cardell spoke on his experience of moving from an academic to a public music library,[2] and I discussed the move from public to academic.[3] The title of the panel, "Crossing the Great Divide," seemed quite appropriate, not because experience has shown a great gulf between academic and public music librarianship—quite the opposite in fact. The perception that there is a great divide between job environments (e.g., public versus academic, academic versus special) and between job categories (e.g., technical versus public services) nevertheless prevails. It's true that there are differences, and it is precisely those differences that can provide the new and interesting challenges so often sought by mid-career music librarians. In terms of job environment, the differences are likely to be in degree or emphasis.

A Comparison of Environments

Serving as a framework in this comparison of public and academic work environments is Ronald Edwards' article, "Migrating to Public Librarianship—Depart on Time to Ensure a Smooth Flight,"[4] which appeared in the Spring 2002 issue of *Library Trends*, devoted to "Midlife Career Decisions of Librarians." Other articles in the issue included ways to energize a career without changing jobs,[5] becoming a chief librarian,[6] moving to a larger academic library or moving between archival and librarian positions,[7] and moving out of libraries altogether.[8] Edwards's article outlined nine areas basic to all types of libraries, such as collection development and internal organization, and then contrasted these areas in academic and public libraries. He clearly believes that there are significant, even drastic, differences between the two environments. I do not.

Interestingly, there is little in the library literature to support either view. Few surveys or descriptive articles discuss differences between public and academic music librarians or libraries or even offer general comparisons between public and academic library environments. Is the division between types of libraries so fundamental as to need no discussion? Or does there exist an implicit assumption so widely held that it goes unnoticed? Given the lack of literature, much of the following is primarily based on personal experience, offered in the hope that music librarians contemplating a mid-career change will find these observations of interest.

Politics

Edwards asserts that public libraries are far more vulnerable to external politics, noting their reliance on funding from governmental agencies. In addition, public libraries' constituents generate such a diverse range of demands that satisfying them is a political minefield. One group may lobby for more attention at the expense of another. Finally, internal politics are greatly complicated by the library board, a body unique to public libraries.[9] The library board can *in theory* influence day-to-day business and policy.[10]

The fact is, publicly funded academic libraries are just as vulnerable to shifting governmental priorities and economics.[11] Perhaps this is not as obvious since funding for academic public institutions occurs at the state level, rather than city or county. Academic libraries also have a range of constituents: music students, administration, faculty, non-music majors, and in many state-funded institutions, the general public. The political pressure to satisfy each clientele exists here, as well. One colleague has put it nicely: While in public libraries the politics are more obvious, academic libraries face the same political pressures from external bodies and internal constituents.

Collection Development

Edwards states that public libraries employ a more transitory manner of collection development than their academic siblings, that they react to immediate demands and have no focus on research or historical collection development. Instead, public libraries' main operational method is to balance the "product mix" of book, video, and CD formats. While Edwards concedes that medium-to-large public libraries may own special collections, he notes that even these tend to change as societal demands shift.[12]

A transitory, fill-the-demand approach to collection development seems to result from a library's size, whether it is academic or public. Smaller academic libraries collect material to support an undergraduate curriculum, often without historical or research responsibility. Yet larger public libraries often have explicit historical collection development requirements placed upon them by a consortium or the state library. The largest public music libraries have existed longer than many academic music libraries[13] and often have fabulous historical collections. If "research collection development" is defined by the acquisition of manuscripts, then certainly most public libraries, along with many academic libraries, do not qualify. However, if it means the acquisition of general materials to support research, large public music libraries easily fall into this category. The difference here between academic and public music libraries is likely to be in the types of music that are emphasized in research-level collection development.

As for high-demand items, aren't academic libraries hit by requests for what their constituents see as high-demand items? And regarding the concern for "product mix," like public libraries, academic libraries must constantly reassess their balance of print, electronic, video, and audio holdings. Edwards's last point, that public libraries' special collections shift in focus according to external pressure,[14] has some validity. Moreover, focus shifts not so much in what is collected but in the value given to these collections by the libraries' governing agencies. Currently, public libraries are experiencing pressure to reduce staff and specialized service points. The elimination of specialized music reference areas can only have detrimental effects on the specialized music collections themselves.[15]

Censorship

Public libraries are more likely to experience objections from constituents about particular materials, but both academic and public libraries are liable to hear patrons' concerns about freedom of speech. Both must show sensitivity to individual clients' objections about collections, speakers, exhibits, or access to specific websites. All professional librarians are bound by a code of ethics that requires them to tread a fine line regarding the ethics of free access to information.[16]

Employment Procedures

The *Library Trends* article criticizes public libraries for inadequately serving diverse populations, such as patrons with limited English, and for not having adequately diverse staffing. These are issues that challenge all libraries. While services are more difficult to compare, in the area of increasing staff diversity, the statistics do not show any one type of library being more successful than another.[17]

Edwards warns that applicants to public libraries should be prepared for outdated, irrelevant written civil service exams. Yet informal conversations with colleagues during the preparation of this chapter revealed no public music librarian who had to take such an exam. Yes, there are lengthy applications and odd paperwork hoops for some government or civil service jobs. However, the academic hiring process is hardly any more straightforward.

Edwards further complains that public libraries require public library experience, "thereby restricting the potential pool of excellent candidates."[18] If this is true, isn't the reverse also likely—that *academic* libraries are asking for *academic experience,* thereby similarly restricting their pool of candidates? Here is where the perception of a "great divide" creates real obstacles. Anyone attempting to cross over from one library environment to another must currently address the perception that experience at one type of library does not translate into relevant experience for the other.

Internal Organization

Edwards states that academic libraries have a flatter, less hierarchical, and more participative organizational structure than public libraries.[19] To my observation, internal organization is more a matter of library *size* than library *type.* Smaller institutions with fewer staff can function in a flatter manner. Larger institutions tend to be more hierarchical, even amid attempts to reorganize into flatter organization models. Large institutions also are likely to have committees to facilitate communication and standardization of procedures across multiple departments. But regardless of a library's appearance on paper, most librarians will agree that the actual power in the workplace flows vertically, and downward.

Compensation

The Edwards article concludes with a warning that traditionally, public library positions pay less and "may not compensate enough for a shift to be worthwhile in the long run."[20] However, the "Profile of Music Library Association Membership" shows that, at least in 1997, salaries for similar job categories—catalogers, public services, generalists—were similar for all types of libraries.[21] Factors affecting salary seem instead to be linked to region, location, experience, administrative responsibilities, and unionization. Benefits such as medical insurance, vacation time, retirement, and tuition reimbursement were not included in the survey.

Professional Development and Activities

The MLA profile looks at some aspects of librarianship that Edwards does not. It uses information from surveys collected in 1997 to test commonly held assumptions about the profession. One assumption, that more academic music librarians have advanced degrees in music, held true, but others did not: "Academic librarians are more likely to have advanced degrees in music than public librarians. Interestingly, this does not translate into difference in professional or scholarly work: there are no differences among any of these groups with regard to scholarly activity."[22] The survey does not address whether or not professional or scholarly activity is *required* of all groups.

It is apparent that the level of support for such activity does differ between academic and public libraries. The latter tend to focus on continuing education—often through internal or locally held workshops— with practical, short-term goals. Academic libraries, perhaps in support of librarians' faculty status or the equivalent, provide quite a bit more funding and time for research, projects for professional organizations, and work toward advanced degrees or certification.

Public Service

Another important area excluded from the *Library Trends* article is public service. Ruth Watanabe, eminent music librarian, scholar, and educator, has eloquently addressed the issue of service, writing, "Most American libraries, both public and academic (except those existing specifically for research or dedicated to public service) have a dual character. Two groups of clients are served side by side. The one group, consisting of young students, music-lovers, and casually interested persons, requires quick, clear answers to questions which may sometimes appear trivial. The other, comprising research students, faculty, and visiting scholars, requires the best attention, care, and efforts of the librarian."[23] Of course, all libraries will have varying proportions of patron types served, but to this respected writer, such patrons are determined by each music library's size and location, rather than by its type.

Crossing the Great Divide

To any experienced music librarian looking for a positive change, a crossover to a different type of library presents benefits to all concerned. In moving from a public to an academic music library, a qualified professional stays within the field and makes good use of prior experience while finding new areas for growth. The new institution benefits from a new librarian already experienced in most job responsibilities, who requires little training and provides new outlooks, new subject knowledge, and the energy that every new employee brings.

As the number of librarians shrinks due to retirement,[24] changes in careers, and smaller numbers of new MLS graduates,[25] it seems sensible for the profession to make the best use of its remaining qualified and motivated members. For music libraries, this may mean considering candidates with less obviously relevant prior experience. Yet upon closer examination, the experience of those music librarians crossing over may provide just the right match in skills, education, and enthusiasm.

Notes

1. David Lesniaski, "Profile of the Music Library Association Membership: Report of the Working Group Surveying Music Library Personnel Characteristics." *Notes* 56, no. 4 (June 2000). See also www.music.indiana.edu/tech_s/mla/person/notesarticle.htm (19 May 2003).

2. Vic Cardell, "Chicken Soup for the Music Librarian's Soul" (Paper presented at the annual meeting of the Music Library Association, Austin, February 2003).

3. Jeanette Casey, "The Game Remains the Same" (Paper presented at the annual meeting of the Music Library Association, Austin, February 2003).

4. Ronald G. Edwards, "Migrating to Public Librarianship: Depart on Time to Ensure a Smooth Flight." *Library Trends* 50, no. 4 (Spring 2002): 631–39.

5. D. L. Montgomery, "Happily Ever After: Plateauing as a Means for Long-Term Career Satisfaction." *Library Trends* 50, no. 4 (Spring 2002): 702–16.

6. C. J. Matthews, "Becoming a Chief Librarian: An Analysis of Transition Stages in Academic Library Leadership" *Library Trends* 50, no. 4 (Spring 2002): 578–602.

7. T. J. Johnson, "Making It to the Major Leagues: Career Movement Between Library and Archival Professions and from Small College to Large University Libraries." *Library Trends* 50, no. 4 (Spring 2002): 614–30.

8. C. B. Zemon, "Midlife Career Choices: How Are They Different from Other Career Choices?" *Library Trends* 50, no. 4 (Spring 2002): 665–72.

9. Edwards, "Migrating," 633.

10. Edwards, "Migrating," 634. However, informal conversation among colleagues reveals that the library board is often a passive body, reacting to measures presented by the library director.

11. Andrew Albanese, "Academic Library Budgets Squeezed by Lowered Revenue," *Library Journal*, 127, no. 19 (15 November 2002): 16.

12. Edwards, "Migrating," 634.

13. Carol June Bradley, *Music Collections in American Libraries: A Chronology* (Detroit: Information Coordinators, 1981).

14. Edwards, 634.

15. M. Carpenter, "Venerable Carnegie Library Booked for Reshuffle," *Post–Gazette.com: The Interactive Edition of the Pittsburgh Post-Gazette* (10 March 2003), www.postEgazette.com/localnews/ (19 May 2003).

16. American Library Association, *Code of Ethics.* http://ala.org (27 May 2003).

17. E. Edwards and W. Fisher, "Trust, Teamwork, and Tokenism: Another Perspective on Diversity in Libraries," *Library Administration & Management* 17, no. 1 (Winter 2003) 21–27.

18. Edwards, "Migrating," 636.

19. Edwards, "Migrating," 638.

20. Edwards, "Migrating," 638.

21. Lesniaski, "Profile."

22. Lesniaski, "Profile."

23. Ruth Watanabe, "The Scholar and the Music Library," in *Modern Music Librarianship,* Alfred Mann, ed. (Stuyvesant, NY: Pendragon Press, 1989): 221.

24. Rebecca T. Lenzini, "The Graying of the Library Profession: A Survey of Our Professional Association and Their Responses," *Searcher* 10, no. 7 (July/August 2002): 88–97.

25. American Library Association, "Recruitment, Retention, and Restructuring: Human Resources in Academic Libraries." A white paper by the Ad Hoc Task Force on Recruitment and Retention Issues. 20 May 2002. http://staging.ala.org/content/navigationmenu/acrl/Issues_and_Advocacy1/Recruiting_to_the_Profession/recruiting–wp.pdf (19 May 2003).

7

Music Librarians
as Library Administrators:
Turning to the Dark Side?

H. Stephen Wright

About a year and a half ago, I became a library administrator. This was no bizarre twist of fate; I actually sought the administrative position I now hold. This was, in some ways, a surprise to some of my colleagues and friends who believed I'd be a music librarian until I retired (or died on the job). To an extent, it was a surprise to me as well, because for many years I had railed against administrators both privately and publicly. I had published editorials attacking administrative attitudes, philosophies, and fads that I viewed as misguided and dangerously prevalent. When I talked to my music library colleagues at professional conferences, I stridently declared that administrators *weren't* librarians and should *not* be considered colleagues. Administrators (as I explained to anyone who would listen) don't answer reference questions, don't select books, don't offer bibliographic instruction, and don't catalog anything, so in what sense of the word could they possibly consider themselves to be librarians? They aren't, I declared; their goals are completely different from ours, and no administrator, however friendly or cooperative, should be considered "one of us." Yet now I am that figure that I once dismissed, and more than a few friends have remarked on what seems to be a supreme irony. Why did I do this? More to the point, why does any music librarian choose this path? I am far from being the only music librarian who has gone into library administration; indeed, I'm the second music librarian at my institution to do so. In fact, I have come to believe that this is a logical (if not wholly predictable) step for a music librarian in mid-career, and it is arguably positive for the profession of music librarianship and for the broader library world.

Is it even a problem that some music librarians choose to pursue positions outside of the music library world? Anecdotal evidence would suggest that many music librarians *would* characterize such career moves as problematic and damaging to the profession. The membership of the Music Library Association has been shrinking for years now. I briefly served on MLA's Membership Committee during the 1990s, and I noted that there was a definite tendency to view MLA's membership, and the profession of music librarianship in general, as an embattled, endangered species. I recall no discussions of *why* this was bad—it was simply accepted as a given that having fewer music librarians in the world couldn't possibly be a good thing. Indeed, there have been cases in which music librarian or music cataloger positions have been eliminated due to budget reductions, and this is certainly a legitimate concern. However, even when a music librarian advances to administrative ranks and his or her previous position is filled, there are still some raised eyebrows, as if some subtle act of disloyalty has been committed. I certainly sensed this, though not in an overt way. Music librarians have a remarkably strong sense of professional identity, perhaps even more so than other kinds of specialized librarians. Consequently there is a highly refined sense of professional loyalty among music librarians and a concomitant sense of bafflement that anyone would *want* to leave.

In 1990, in the prototype for the present book, Jaclyn Facinelli wrote "Why Music Librarians Leave the Field," which included the results of a survey that explored the reasons that music librarians offered for choosing to move into non-music-oriented library positions. Of course, Facinelli's research wasn't limited to music librarians who pursued administrative positions; some of her respondents moved laterally within their institutions or left the library profession entirely. Nevertheless, the reasons that these survey participants cited are quite compelling, and there were definitely similar circumstances in my own situation. Perhaps the most compelling factor that Facinelli discovered was the problematic nature of advancement in the music library profession. At conferences and in online discussions, music librarians have expressed grave concerns about people "leaving the field," but the singular and highly circumscribed nature of the profession virtually guarantees an almost constant exodus.

Music librarians entering the field upon leaving graduate school have a range of options. They can seek positions at institutions having a single music librarian and immediately immerse themselves in the whole range of duties associated with music librarianship: answering reference queries, developing a collection, cataloging scores and sound recordings, supervising a staff, etc. Others may join a configuration of "subject specialists" who also share some general duties. Still others may start their careers as music catalogers; such positions are often considered entry-level This is exactly what happened in my case when I entered the field in the early 1980s. Indeed, many music librarians of similar vintage started their careers as catalogers, because that's all that was available. The field seemed to be glutted with qualified, aspiring music librarians in those years, and many of my colleagues began their careers with insecure "soft money" cataloging positions or as sabbatical replacements. (My first job was a permanent cataloging position, so I felt quite fortunate compared to my "soft-money" friends.) Finally, some newly minted music librarians start as junior members of the staffs in large, complex music libraries at major universities or in the music departments of big-city public libraries. This latter option is particularly attractive because it offers tremendous opportunities for mentoring and professional development; this was a particular concern in the pre-Internet days when music librarians often complained of feeling isolated. It also offers the psychological boost of working at a prestigious institution, which is no small matter to many music librarians. One of the characteristics of the profession that I noticed early in my career is that many music librarians are eager to work at the more celebrated, high-status institutions and will often accept lower salaries and poor working conditions to do so.

Once a music librarian has been in the field for roughly a decade, the complexion of his or her career development tends to change—often dramatically. The ten-year anniversary, often celebrated with plaques and other symbols, seems to be a time of reevaluation for many. In my case I noted a particularly striking detail. I started my preadministrative position (as music librarian at Northern Illinois University) in the summer of 1985. Ten years earlier, I had just graduated from high school! Now, fast-forward to the summer of 1995. Ten years before that, I was sitting at the same desk, *in the same chair*, doing the same job. Obviously, one's thoughts turn to career changes at such times.

Another issue, which Facinelli also took care to note, is that music librarians' personal circumstances tend to change in predictable ways as they age.[1] People may want to stay in the music library profession, but they may not want to relocate—or simply *cannot* relocate. Librarians just starting their careers tend to be much more mobile; they have few possessions, may not have spouses or partners, and are generally less "settled" and more adaptable to transitory living situations. (I once heard this described as the "cats and apartments" phase of life.) After about ten years, the music librarian may have a family and a mortgage, and a stable lifestyle seems much more appealing. The librarian's spouse or partner, if any, probably has a job that he or she is reluctant to abandon; in the case of academic librarians, the partner probably has a job at the university as well. Finally, the whole idea of *moving*, once an adventure, now seems profoundly distasteful.

Unfortunately, unless the music librarian lives in a megalopolis like Chicago or Los Angeles, staying in the profession and staying in the same city will probably be mutually exclusive. The music library world can essentially be viewed as a pyramid; at the broad base of that pyramid are countless small- and medium-sized libraries that employ one or two music librarians who are often hired on an entry-level basis. As one ascends this pyramid toward larger and more sophisticated music libraries, the range of opportunities shrinks. There may be enough entry-level positions to absorb the output of the few music librarianship training programs, but if one wants a leadership position guiding one of the major music collections, the pickings become alarmingly slim indeed. There are hundreds of people in the Music Library Association, but there are definitely not hundreds of Indianas or Eastmans. The implication is that music librarians must either begin competing with the best and the brightest in the field for a handful of prestigious jobs (and be inured to the idea of moving) or leave the field for something new. That "something new" will, in many cases, turn out to be an administrative job.

Why, though, would a music librarian *want* to be a library administrator? The mere idea of this seemed repugnant to me at one time; it was analogous to Luke Skywalker turning to the dark side of the Force. Facinelli quotes some of the reasons that her survey participants gave, and when I first read her chapter back in 1990, some of these reasons sounded like empty platitudes to me. "My work is more varied . . . more universal," one said. Another said, "I am looking at a bigger picture." Still another made the expansive claim, "I am now part of the future."[2]

Writing this in 2003, I understand these statements a bit better, although I would not express them this way. Rather, I would use an artistic analogy: the music librarian who becomes an administrator is working on a larger canvas. The detailed, pointillistic brushwork of correcting uniform titles, looking up composer dates, and finding sources for obscure compact discs has given way to broad strokes on a mural. If a musical analogy is preferable, it is the difference between playing a solo instrument and conducting an orchestra.

Facinelli also provides this intriguing quote from one of her survey participants: "I felt I could do a better job administering than those who were in it." From my 1990 perspective, this seemed almost petty and suggested that the speaker worked in an unusually dysfunctional environment. However, I later had a similar kind of epiphany as my experience and knowledge grew; I realized that the administrators who seemed so lofty and omniscient when I was a new librarian were just people like me, albeit older. They had no secret knowledge that made them better or smarter than I was. Perhaps their additional experience, and the knowledge gained through that experience, gave them a broader frame of reference than the frontline librarians, but that was all. I realized then, and still know now, that library administrators are not intrinsically more intelligent or talented than a reference librarian, bibliographer, or cataloger.

Any librarian has the potential to become an administrator, and library administrators have emerged from every aspect of library work. However, as I prepared to move into my new position, I came to believe that as a music librarian I was especially well-prepared to assume administrative duties, and I still believe passionately that music librarians make the best library administrators. This isn't just blind loyalty to my professional roots; music librarians, due to the unique nature of their duties, are marvelously suited to the administrative role. The most obvious advantage is that many music librarians have been running their own libraries for years. The typical music library is a microcosm of a larger, more general library; the librarian therein has usually handled all of the various facets of library work, including circulation, reference, collection development, bibliographic instruction, and cataloging. The music librarian often has been managing a staff and has tended to the routine matters of making sure a library opens and closes on time and has reliable, properly trained employees. He or she has dealt with the entire spectrum of librarianship, from the most exalted philosophical issues to the most mundane matters of carpeting and air conditioning. Who indeed knows more about more aspects of librarianship than a music librarian?

One could, of course, argue that any head of a branch library is just as well prepared for administrative tasks, and although branch music libraries are common in the academic world there are many other kinds of branch libraries as well. Nevertheless, I maintain that the music librarian has one advantage that other librarians do not have—a deep and profound understanding and appreciation of the pivotal role that cataloging plays in the library world. It is often said that if you can catalog music, you can catalog anything, because music cataloging is ferociously complex. Furthermore, the profligacy of the major classical composers ensures that music librarians must have a thorough understanding of how authority control can tame very large arrays of related bibliographic entities. The music librarian is thus compelled to have (or develop) an eye for detail, and the music librarian who becomes an administrator retains that appreciation for the importance of that detail, even if he or she is now working in broader strokes. Throughout my career I have noted that the weakest and least respected administrators were always those who had no understanding and appreciation of cataloging. That lack of understanding often manifested itself in a general contempt for the countless meticulous and sometimes tedious tasks that are necessary in library work. The music-librarian-turned-administrator is far less likely to fall into this trap.

I would also argue that having music librarians become administrators is good for music librarianship in general, because administrators are usually in a position to implement things that a frontline music librarian cannot, and music libraries can undoubtedly benefit from this. One of my first actions as a newly minted administrator was to order a replacement for the aging theft-detection system in the Northern Illinois University music library. I had been begging for a new system for years, because the library's existing model was so old that the manufacturer could not provide replacement parts and the factory technicians were refusing to even look at it. Perhaps I was guilty of favoritism, and perhaps I would have gotten the replacement system eventually if I had stayed in the music library—but the point is that my background gave me a real understanding of the music library's needs, and my administrative position gave me the power to act on those needs. It can only help music librarianship in general if we have administrators who are sympathetic to our goals.

When I attend MLA conferences now, I'm typically asked if I miss being a music librarian. In my case, the answer is no. I would not be so presumptuous as to assume that every former music librarian would feel this way; this is a deeply personal issue. I believed that I had done enough in the music library, and indeed was starting to feel as if I had run out of ideas. We hired a new music librarian who brought fresh ideas and youthful energy to the job, and I have had no desire to hover over him or micromanage him. Obviously some music librarians leave the field and want to return later; Facinelli quoted some of them, and their emotions are perfectly valid.

At conferences, I'm also asked what being an administrator is like. When I'm in a more serious mood, I generally say that it's a very political sort of job; I have to balance many competing interests and build consensus so that the library can move forward. My days of taking dogmatic, extreme positions are over. I must also watch what I say very carefully. When I was a music librarian, I could (citing academic freedom) blurt out whatever incendiary thoughts came into my head, and I relished my role as anarchist and rabble-rouser. Now, the slightest off-hand or sardonic remark in an elevator or hallway can set the rumor mill into motion and escalate into a juggernaut of misinformation. I must choose my words carefully and craft every e-mail to be absolutely clear and unambiguous.

When I'm in a more jocular mood, I say that being an administrator is like having a big target painted on your back. It is a given that people are going to get angry at you—not only because it is impossible to please everyone, but also because you must occasionally support and implement unpopular policies that you may not like or agree with. In some cases these policies may be dictated by high-level university officials that your library staff doesn't know and has never met. It accomplishes nothing to protest that you're only doing what the president or provost has decreed, and indeed it is politically foolish to shift blame upwards. Your librarians and staff will get mad at you simply because you're there and because you're a convenient target. Administrators are paid more than other librarians are, and one library director I knew aptly described this additional compensation as "hazard pay."

Surprisingly, I have found that my musical background provides an ideal managerial model. I studied conducting in graduate school, and although my dreams of conducting the London Symphony Orchestra never materialized, I can apply my conducting experience every day as a library administrator. A conductor must follow the written score—analogous to the library's mission—but also provides a unique interpretive vision of that work and can choose to emphasize particular elements. The conductor must also blend the individual sounds of many unique and strong-willed musicians to produce a coherent whole; the library administrator must achieve a similar coherence with librarians who each have their own singular and sometimes passionate viewpoint. Yet the conductor must never micromanage the orchestra; a conductor who continually brings rehearsals to a halt to tell the clarinetist what fingering to use or to instruct the timpanist in how to hold the sticks will quickly and deservedly incur the orchestra's hostility and frustration. So it is with the library administrator: one must provide an overarching vision while leaving the details up to the creativity and intelligence of each librarian.

Music librarianship is sometimes viewed by its practitioners as a nebulous "cause," like preserving the rainforest or protecting pandas from extinction. It isn't; it's a profession, a job that would be meaningless without the context of the larger world of library users and music literature. Music librarianship is an inextricable subset of the universe of librarianship, the profession that seeks to collect, organize, preserve, and provide access to the record of human knowledge. It does no harm for music librarians to become library administrators; there is no abandonment of our principles in such career changes. Rather, the music librarian who moves into administration will inevitably have opportunities to benefit music librarianship in new and more expansive ways; these opportunities may not be frequent, but when they do appear they will truly matter. Until there are enough professional positions to allow every music librarian to advance to the summit of the pyramid—a scenario that is obviously impossible—the practitioners of music librarianship should never be discouraged from entering the administrative ranks, because by doing so they can help propagate our ideals into a vast and influential world.

Notes

1. Jaclyn Facinelli, "Why Music Librarians Leave," in *Careers in Music Librarianship: Perspectives from the Field,* comp. Carol Tatian, MLA Technical Report, 18. (Canton, MA: Music Library Association, 1991), 57–66.

2. Facinelli, "Why Music Librarians Leave," 65.

8

Tomorrow's Music Librarians

Ned Quist

The art of prophecy is very difficult, especially with regard to the future.
—attributed to Mark Twain[1]

Looking into the future rarely yields profound insights; rather it is often educated guesses built on previous experience. The experience offered here is that of an academic music librarian, currently the most prevalent kind of music librarian, but not necessarily so in the future. The educated guesses are those of one who has served his profession largely in private institutions of higher learning where resources, though rarely sumptuous, are at least reasonably consistent. They are consistent enough that looking into the future is not a discouraging practice but rather a useful and often successful pastime combining hope, potential, and a great deal of good fortune, some of which comes to all of us at one time or another.

This vision of the future presents the package of professional issues, educational needs, and required skills that music librarians are soon likely to encounter. It also speculates on the activites that will be the daily work of music librarians in the not too distant future.

The Issues

Four major considerations face music librarians in the immediate future. Fundamentally, they can be recognized as issues that have always concerned us. But rapid changes—in formats, in our spaces, in questions of intellectual ownership, and in our users—require a long and respectful look.

Format

Unlike the libraries that support most disciplines, those that support music have always dealt with more than just books. In fact, one may point to the presence of printed music as at least one of the historical reasons that music libraries came to exist as separate entities. Once music libraries began collecting sound recordings and other media they became places where periodic change was the norm.

In the case of sound recordings, music librarians have dealt with format change every ten to twenty years, beginning with the seventy-eight rpm record, collected from the 1930s onward until the introduction of the digital compact disc in the early 1980s. Now the arrival of MP3, via file sharing services such as KaZaa and the catalogs of streamed audio offered by some recording companies, seems to be leading to a total eradication of the physical formats. Yet the introduction of two new formats, SACD and DVD-A, suggest that recording companies have not yet surrendered the notion of marketing physical objects, albeit the new formats will likely be protected from easy duplication. Video materials, likewise, have undergone several changes of format since their relatively recent introduction into music libraries in the 1980s. Although online streaming of shorter video "clips" has been available for some time, the wide availability of longer video productions, will likely follow. Music librarians of the past learned through hard-won experience that poor choices in the adoption of a new format can have serious consequences. Ask any who invested heavily in 8-track tapes or 12-inch video discs. The musical score, perhaps the first "nonbook" format collected by libraries, is also beginning to move to electronic form, but not in the same fashion as recordings. As currently distributed online, scores must be printed and put on the music stand. Electronic music stands have just begun to appear on the market and, if successful, may offer a way to completely reduce the dependence on a printed paper version for performance.[2] Instead, we may see distribution of an actual electronic score, readable on the electronic stand.

Journals in music are increasingly appearing online either as part of aggregated packages from such vendors as Ebsco, Chadwyck-Healey, and Project MUSE, or individually, such as the journals from Cambridge, Oxford, and California university presses. In these early years of the new millennium, the availability of large backfiles of significant journals has already begun to play a major role, as many libraries both public and academic have found it necessary to cancel print subscriptions or to move large runs of printed journals to remote storage facilities. Likewise, books and dissertations are appearing increasingly in electronic form.

These transitions in formats for music materials pose new and significant questions to future music librarians: How will music librarians handle an increasingly electronic library, much of which will not reside in the music library itself but on remote servers?

Specifically, how will the digitization of music libraries affect their space requirements and the use of existing space? How will issues of intellectual property affect digitization, and who will the users be in this new environment?

Space

The way space is allocated for music materials, particularly in academic libraries, may shift significantly in the coming years. Audio and video streaming of reserve music materials, whether through a licensed vendor or through each library's initiative to create and stream its own digital files, has generated the potential for much traditional library activity to now take place outside the library walls. The additional availability of electronic music encyclopedias (such as www.grovemusic.com), large indexes of music literature (such as Music Index and RILM), and full-text journals and e-books has made it possible for many university students to do much of their research from their dorm rooms or homes rather than in the library itself. Furthermore, as academic library space becomes harder to find and the expense of building new space less likely, many libraries have begun storing substantial portions of their collections in remote storage facilities. All of these suggest a need to rethink the use of the space that libraries now have.

The complexities of the growing online environment for music and music research suggest that more space be dedicated to instruction in the use of these resources. In addition, as music libraries begin to participate in the creation of digital libraries, either cooperatively or individually, they will need production space to create, edit, test, and deliver multimedia files and to scan public domain scores, fragile books, and unique primary source materials, including photographs and manuscripts. And if the trend toward more powerful yet smaller computing devices continues, we may also soon see a day when music libraries need no longer dedicate space to banks of large computers but instead rely more on the availability of smaller portable devices including "tablet" computers and handheld listening and viewing devices in a wireless network environment. All of these changes lead one to hope for a future in which the library need no longer be a hectic "info-arcade" where information is "consumed" but can again be a place where research and study become reacquainted with quiet reflection.

Intellectual Property

Hanging over all of these movements toward technological developments in music libraries is the shadow of intellectual property. Music librarians are at the same time the servants and the servers of intellectual property. In order to serve their patrons, they must negotiate the often slippery path of balancing the legitimate needs of patrons with the property rights of the publishers, composers, performers, editors, and authors whose intellectual property they collect, interpret, and disseminate. The increasing use of digital resources, and the need of many libraries to create them where they don't yet exist commercially, has put many music libraries somewhat ahead of the industry, and this is a risky legal position. Perhaps if the future includes a music industry that distributes its products entirely or mostly electronically (protected by various electronic watermarks, copy protection schemes, and licenses), the future music librarian may become more an interpreter and less a digitizer of physical objects. Yet even then music librarians must be archivists of these ephemeral products that could easily disappear from their publishers' servers as their market value diminishes over time.

This great revolution in the world of intellectual property also holds some potential rewards for libraries that own (and own the rights to) unique musical resources, whether they are the unpublished writings of an arcane Russian music theorist, the snapshots of a local jazz musician, or the homemade tapes of an internationally known recording star. Libraries can legitimately become publishers of digital content if they astutely secure the intellectual property rights to archival material at the time of its acquisition. As digital libraries grow into maturity, the online publication of such materials, together with the added value of contextual interpretation by the music librarians themselves, offers great potential not only for enriching the scholarly community but perhaps for modest profit as well.

Library Users

Until the 21st century, music libraries, whether public or academic, had a great deal in common. They all contained core collections of music reference books, scores, and recordings that largely reflected the canon of Western art music. But the future could bring an increased specialization as different types of libraries move to capitalize on those technologies most appropriate for their users. A public library serving a clientele primarily interested in popular and world music may take a very different approach from a music school library serving primarily a community of performers or a university music department serving a very focused group of scholars. A large state university music school serving all of these populations may take yet another path. Perhaps more than ever before, our future music librarians will need to decide who their customers are and what kind of music collection they need.

Here is one scenario: A public library in a major city, pressed for space and resources, may decide to discard its collection of little-used scores and recordings of Western art music and focus its efforts instead on collecting and digitizing music of local musicians. This will likely include music of cultures not previously collected, such as Chinese, Southeast Asian, Latin American, and African immigrant cultures. It may continue to offer a greatly reduced circulating collection of book, score, and recorded materials but rely on a subscription to an online library of e-books, a prepaid block of online sheet music downloads, and a license with an online streaming audio vendor for the rest. Supplementing the commercial services purchased by the library would be an increasing number of public domain materials digitized by other libraries and freely available over the web.

Education for New Environments

Librarians will need to continue to be active participants in the musical culture, as performers and scholars, curious listeners and audience members. As always, they will need to know music from the inside, not just from a listing in a catalog, in a database, or on a website. This knowledge, along with a variety of other innate and acquired abilities, may prove more valuable than formal education. The graduate degree in library science (or in music) as the basic credential has already begun to loosen a bit as a hard and fast requirement, but in management positions it will likely remain paramount for some time.

Clearly the fields of music performance and scholarship are in a state of great flux. The music of Bach, Beethoven, and Brahms remains at the traditional core of most academic programs, but the music of the Beatles, Notorious B.I.G., Art Blakey, and Orchestra Baobab plays a major role not only in the public libraries of the future but also in the libraries of academe. Learning to build a collection that includes a broad sampling of music from Liverpool in the 1960s, the rap world of the 1990s, the hard bop world of the 1950s, or world music in the early years of the new millennium is a new responsibility, one that few library schools or music schools have yet addressed in a systematic way. Through the application of sociological techniques to the study of music, the boundaries between art music and popular music blur, and interdisciplinary approaches become more important. Necessarily broadening the scope of music study are new fields or relationships within music, including such disciplines as gender studies, semiotics, and iconography.

Whether in the future we continue to collect physical items or digital ones, we must still possess the critical acumen to evaluate and select those things most appropriate for the clientele we serve. As Michael Gorman observes, "Our job [as librarians] is not to be an emergency management agency for the flood of information. Our job—the heart of our job—is to organize the world of learning so that people can profit from it."[3] Essential to these efforts must be a willingness on the part of the future music librarian not only to master the critical literature of print media but also to locate and utilize the often ephemeral and elusive reviews of new music that spring up continuously on the Internet and in the underground press.

As reference service shifts from face-to-face encounters to more online encounters, music librarians of the future will employ a new array of techniques and technologies. In response to music information inquiries submitted electronically, reference librarians will provide online sessions and visual and aural demonstrations to their remote patrons.

Here is another scenario: A library patron sends an instant message to the music reference librarian requesting help with a research paper that the patron is writing on a local composer. After some back-and-forth messages—a digital reference interview—the librarian decides the patron would benefit from a number of electronic resources as well as print materials that the library holds. Quickly dragging and dropping a number of digital objects, including URLs of relevant online indexes, e-books, digitized scores, and recordings, the librarian assembles a customized portal for the patron's project while the patron watches from her computer screen. Several follow-up messages explain how to use and cite these resources. The librarian shows the patron thumbnails of some of the images and plays a couple of the audio files to confirm that these in fact meet the patron's needs.

Once and Future Skills

The skill set the of the well-rounded music librarian of the future will likely include a mix of traditional library and academic skills as well as a variety of new ones. Traditional skills include foreign language expertise, ability to read music, and experience as a performing artist. A graduate degree in library science will continue to be valued, though perhaps in different ways.[4] Application of research methods, or a systematic approach to finding information, remains an essential skill, although traditional approaches will change with the availability of digital libraries and data mining techniques. In addition to an increasing number of Internet-based resources, in-house databases containing information of local interest will require the mastery of specific techniques for each search engine or the creation or licensing of meta-search software to search across them. Among the many skills likely to be valued in the future of the profession are the ability to teach, the willingness to tackle technical issues with "legacy" equipment and formats, and the political savvy to keep the music collection vital to the organization.

Languages, Verbal and Musical

Beyond the languages of Western Europe traditionally valued in music scholarship, foreign languages will become more significant as academic curricula and public interest in world music grow. The need for language ability will increase as music libraries specialize in musics reflecting the interests of their diverse local communities. The ability to read music will continue to be valuable as long as musicians continue to rely upon the core repertoire of Western music and on the traditional system of music notation. Experience as a performer provides not only an empathetic approach to patrons who are performers but provides the skills needed to interpret musical notation for patrons unable to do so.

Teaching

As our information systems become more complex, comprising a web of print resources, legacy formats such as LPs, CDs, and videotapes, free and licensed resources on the Internet, and digital libraries, our patrons will need to become more sophisticated in their use. While we would like to think that they can acquire the necessary skills in schools and university classrooms, past experience has shown this not to be the case. As the people closest to this web of information, librarians will teach their patrons, including teachers and faculty, the new skills necessary to successfully find information needed for performance, research, and instruction in music. This is likely to include instruction in creating custom electronic resources to navigate, analyze, and evaluate what they find.

Familiarity with Legacy Equipment

Digital libraries will grow, as resources permit, at various speeds in a number of places. But for many years to come, legacy formats (including all the physical formats we now consider contemporary) will need to be preserved at least in academic and research libraries. Before they can be digitized, most legacy formats need to be played back on a variety of equipment, which, given a growing scarcity of parts and equipment, will become increasingly difficult to maintain. As of this writing, CD and DVD players are still ubiquitous, but already cassette decks, reel-to-reel tape players, and especially early 12-inch video disc players are becoming difficult to find and repair. The music librarian of the future will deal with the preservation of both the original media and their original playback equipment.

Political Savvy

Budget cuts, reorganizations, and changes in the makeup of the music library's primary clientele all influence the perceived importance of the music collection. To preserve the viability of the music library, the future music librarian will be skillful at forming alliances, networking with administration and colleagues, and building strong relationships with the library's users. Visibility—in the form of public relations, exhibits, successful cultivation of donors, and grant writing—will serve to keep the music collection viable and vital to its community of users. A savvy librarian's delicate combination of skills will provide the users of music collections with a growing and dynamic array of musical content and attendant services.

The Music Library in
the Larger Library World

Music libraries rarely exist in a vacuum, but rather as a part of larger library systems, whether public or academic. As part of larger systems they can alternately benefit and suffer from changes in management styles, new technologies, and theoretical concepts that influence library operations. Here, it is essential that the music librarian remain aware of the trends in library management, technology, and information management that play such a large role in the larger library community, for sooner or later they will have an effect on the services and collections of the music library. Ignoring such trends will threaten to marginalize the music library. Three general library issues facing music librarians in the near future concern integrated systems, metadata, and institutional reorganization.

Integrated Systems

The next generation of integrated library systems will include access to print and electronic media through a single "portal." The emphasis will likely be on really "full text," including literary texts, pictorial texts (still and motion picture), musical texts (both visual and aural), and texts born in electronic form. Some currently available products already offer a means of searching not only the digital holdings of the home library but also licensed resources (reference databases, full text aggregators, e-journals). What remains to be seen is how these products, or their homegrown counterparts, will affect the future of the online catalog, which traditionally has been the main resource for most libraries. Will they exist alongside the online catalog, absorb it, or replace it altogether?

Metadata

Various metadata standards will profoundly change music cataloging as it existed in the twentieth century. It might be said that cataloging is quickly *becoming* metadata. The cataloging record, perhaps the original metadata, is now merging with record structures created in various other fields of endeavor to provide increased access to new kinds of information. Metadata, including more than just descriptive text, may encompass digital file structure, copyright ownership or license restrictions, and behavior in various environments. The tasks of composing the metadata may be all or partly automated but may also fall to several persons in a distributed workflow. Catalogers of the future will need to move confidently between different record formats and standards and will increasingly make use of data provided by sources outside the cataloging field and even outside the library field.

Institutional Reorganization

Reorganizations of library structure (whether to change the focus of library services or to save money) will affect the traditional way music libraries have operated and who operates them. Recent cases of restructuring in public libraries have done away with separate music departments, dispersing recordings to media divisions and scores to the general stacks. Music librarians have taken on more general duties and other reference librarians have been "cross trained" in handling music reference queries. Similarly, in academic libraries, team or team-like structures are moving away from traditional hierarchical management structures in order to achieve maximum flexibility among dwindling numbers of library staff. As in public libraries, reassignments are being made to favor flexibility rather than specialization. Job descriptions are changing to reflect this new reality.

Summary

The issues facing the future of music librarianship may be daunting, but music librarians have routinely faced change in the materials they handle and interpret. Digitization certainly offers new challenges, particularly in the area of intellectual property, but issues of licensing and permissions seem to be getting easier rather than harder, although their economic impact on the resources of the music library remains to be seen. Perhaps a bigger challenge is that of engaging newly created works in digital form and bringing them to our users in an organized and understandable context. This will require new efforts as librarians become creators of contextual content (introductions, electronic portals) and progressively informed teachers. This traditional role will become more necessary and more central to the music librarian's activity.

Clearly, music librarians will need to keep abreast of the music industry and the field of library science. Profound changes in library service, management styles, and technologies will influence the future music library's operation. Always far more than mere custodians, more than ever music librarians will be interpreters, teachers, and perhaps creators of new content as well.

Much of what the future practitioners of this profession will need to know will not be taught in library schools or music schools but will grow out of the inquisitiveness of the committed professional. Music librarians of the future will be persons of endless curiosity. They will be tenacious in pursuit of funding and the opportunities presented by technology. They will be willing and able to learn new skills. They will be opportunistic for the benefit of their users and for their collections and creative in their ability to promote, collect, develop, and interpret the musical resources in the library of the future. Most of all, they will continue in the long tradition of music librarians who have welcomed change and made it work to the advantage of their libraries' patrons.

Notes

1. Kim A. McDonald, "Many of Mark Twain's Famed Humorous Sayings are Found to Have Been Misattributed to Him," *Chronicle of Higher Education* 38, no. 2 (4 September 1991): A8.

2. See www.estand.com and www.vivaldistudio.com/Eng/VivaScores.asp for some of the current efforts in this area. (12 March 2003).

3. Michael Gorman, "The Library Shall Endure: A Conversation with Michael Gorman," in *The Book & The Computer: Online Symposium,* www.honco.net/os/gorman.html (12 March 2003).

4. See www.musiclibraryassoc.org/pdf/Core_Competencies.pdf (12 March 2003) for a forward-looking view of the traditional skills music librarians are expected to possess.

9

The Music Library Association

Laura Dankner

The Music Library Association, the largest of all national music library groups, is the organization of choice for those who work with music collections in a variety of institutional settings throughout the United States. Music librarians do, of course, often have other professional affiliations as well, either library- or music-based. While these other groups are certainly important, for music subject specificity MLA will always remain the most useful of all American professional library organizations. Through regional chapters, annual meetings, publications, and other services, MLA offers a broad spectrum of practical information and professional support uniquely tailored to the needs and interests of music specialists in libraries.

Founded in 1931 by a small but determined group of music librarians and musicologists,[1] MLA has grown in stature and size over the years. MLA is governed by a member-elected board of directors, which includes the president. While MLA pays for the services of a professional management firm and a few members receive modest honorariums for special services rendered to the organization, the association is largely volunteer-run. To this end, MLA's organizational structure includes a wealth of committees, task forces, working groups, and roundtables. Virtually all members who wish to be active participants in MLA's governance structure find it possible to become involved through membership in these various groups, which run the gamut from the role-specific (e.g., bibliographic control, education, reference and public service, collection development committees) to the subject specific (e.g., black music, popular and jazz, composers' and performers' roundtables, to name just a few). MLA's committees work year-round, often communicating by electronic means, and also have space on MLA's annual meeting program. They plan and execute projects, present occasional publications or position papers, and may serve as MLA's liaisons to other organizations.

The national Association's structure also provides oversight for its active publication schedule, which includes *Notes*, the influential scholarly journal, the web-based *MLA Newsletter*, the monthly *Music Cataloging Bulletin*, and several monographic series. While not an official organ of the national organization, MLA-L, an electronic mail distribution list, helps members and nonmembers alike with day-to-day library issues and provides news about legislative initiatives of special interest to musicians and librarians. To this last end, MLA's legislation committee provides a most valuable service not only by MLA-L postings but also through the committee's copyright website, one of MLA's most visited web pages, accessed through MLA's own official website.[2] In fact, readers should always consult this site for the most current information regarding who we are and what we do.

MLA meetings are rotated among geographic locations throughout the country. These annual meetings, generally held in early to mid-winter, are brimming with professional growth opportunities through workshops, plenary sessions, and other programmatic meetings. It is also the time when committees meet to discuss past activities and plan future projects. Professional exhibits are an important feature of these get-togethers. Publishers, vendors of books, scores, audiovisual, and electronic products, and purveyors of a variety of library-related materials are all well represented, and the exhibitors are happy to spend time with current or prospective clients explaining, and demonstrating their products and services. The MLA display showcases current publications and, to benefit the Association's activities, the MLA shop sells MLA-themed merchandise. The Development Committee's Marketing Subcommittee and many volunteers run the shop. For many conference attendees, the MLA display and shop and the top-quality professional vendor exhibits are a high point of the meeting.

MLA's annual business meeting, presided over by the president, traditionally closes the annual meeting. This event includes the announcement of the winners of MLA's several publication and research awards, Freeman travel award recipients, and possible special citation and/or special achievement awards, if either have been issued for the year just past. These meetings also serve to inform the membership about the progress of MLA's fund-raising initiatives (coordinated through the Development Committee) and, when necessary, also include brief remembrances of recently deceased members. The meeting traditionally ends with information about the next annual meeting, with the program chair and the local arrangements chair(s) inviting all to attend. In addition to the extremely busy program agenda, the annual meeting features social events as well, including an opening reception held in the exhibit area, the president's reception, to which all members with official MLA responsibilities are invited, and the final banquet. There are often additional events as well, such as local concerts and receptions, allowing for a good time—and good networking opportunities—for all.

MLA's regional chapters also allow for active member participation and are especially important for those whose personal or professional situation doesn't always allow for regular attendance or even membership at the national level. The larger chapters even mirror MLA's organizational structure with working committees and other activities, but whatever the chapters' various projects, they all provide an important support role in the professional lives of their members. Chapter information, complete with website URLs and contact information, is available through the national website.

Through the organizational structure, publications, services, and meetings, the Association is able to serve its members' diverse professional interests. From the cataloger to the reference librarian, the branch librarian and the administrator—and increasingly, for those who serve in a multiplicity of professional roles—MLA can play an important role throughout a professional lifetime. Here are some more specific examples of how MLA serves its members during these various career stages.

MLA is committed to educating students about careers in music librarianship and assisting students in securing their initial jobs in the profession. This goal is accomplished in a variety of ways. On the chapter level, members may visit local library schools to speak with students about career options and may help fund students' attendance at a regional meeting, as mentioned below.

The national MLA website provides access to several publications that are particularly useful for students and prospective music librarians. These include a brochure on careers (*Music Librarianship: Is it for You?*)

and an online version of the MLA Membership brochure. The Education
Committee publishes the *Directory of Library School Offerings in Music
Librarianship*, and the Committee's Library School Liaison subcommittee
is responsible for the very useful Core Competencies of Music Librarians,
which is essential reading for anyone considering a music library career
or considering employing a music specialist in an institution.

Students or newcomers who wish to get a preview of what MLA is
about can often attend a regional chapter meeting or even the national
meeting. Several chapters provide monetary support for attendance at a
regional meeting and often publish information on how to secure funding
on their websites. The national MLA offers the Freeman Travel Award,
designed for students or those in the beginning of their music library
careers who haven't yet attended a national meeting. MLA's publication
and research-oriented awards include the Walter Gerboth award, which
is specifically designed for MLA national members in the first five years
of their careers, and which assists "research-in-progress in music or music
librarianship."[3]

The Placement Service, with its monthly *Job List* appearing on the
MLA website, publishes the most complete national listing of positions
involving music responsibilities available. The placement officer also
coordinates a mentoring program for the annual meeting, which pairs
newcomers with experienced practitioners. This very successful service
has done much to help those attending their first national MLA feel almost
immediately comfortable within the organization. An informal
newcomers' orientation meeting, hosted by the Membership Committee,
is followed by a first-time-attendees' reception, made possible by the
generosity of the Wicker Foundation, whose financial support helps
sponsor this event.

Throughout the early and mid-career years, MLA members find much
useful practical career assistance through their active participation in
MLA at the chapter and national level. Whether in person at meetings or
virtually via the Internet, they meet their colleagues in similar
organizational settings and discuss common problems and concerns. They
keep abreast of new and developing issues in the profession through
attendance at annual meeting preconference workshops and at plenary
and other sessions, which are part of the annual meeting program.

They keep current on their professional reading through publications
such as *Notes* for important articles on a variety of topics, for the
comprehensive book and score reviews, and for the innovative columns.
They consult monographs in the Basic Manual Series, which, as the

overall title suggests, is a compendium of useful information on a wide variety of topics.[4] As more volumes are published in this MLA-sponsored series, they are sure to become mainstays to everyone responsible for facets of the management of music collections in a variety of institutional settings. They also read monographs that appear in the other MLA-sanctioned series.

A Basic Music Library, a joint ALA-MLA publication, while not always suitable for current ordering information (having been published a few years ago) remains an important collection development tool, including listings of essential music library materials. The Placement Service, of course, remains useful to members at all stages of their careers, since the *Job List* includes positions suitable for experienced librarians as well as for relative newcomers.

Members in academic settings often find professional involvement in MLA crucial to the tenure or continuing appointment procedures at their institutions. While service on committees is one possibility, another avenue is through writing. There are ample possibilities for all members who wish to write for publication within MLA's publishing programs, from articles in chapter newsletters up through and including publication of major articles in the juried journal *Notes* or authorship of a monograph in an MLA series. Of course publishing opportunities aren't limited to members in academe, since many in public, conservatory, and special library settings are certainly well represented as authors in MLA's various publication ventures.

This is also true of involvement in MLA's governance structure. While the president appoints all committee chairs, subchairs, and members, anyone interested in service is encouraged to contact the committee chair or the president to express this interest. Sooner or later most members are appointed to committees of preference. This situation is due in some degree to MLA's relatively small size and, most important, to MLA's participatory, volunteer-based organizational structure. It isn't at all uncommon for a relative newcomer in the profession to be appointed to a national-level committee or subcommittee within a very few years of his or her membership in MLA.

In mid- and late career, MLA remains an important resource. Members in this stage may find fulfillment in assuming the chair of an MLA committe, may perhaps be asked to stand for election to the Board, or may be issued a special achievement award or a citation. Or they may choose to continue their previous level of service as committee members, roundtable participants, or active chapter supporters. Retired members are welcome to continue in an active role. MLA offers retiree as well as student membership levels, at a reduced cost.

But there's also another side of MLA that at least for this particular music librarian becomes especially important as the autumnal career phase looms. I've already outlined what I hope are compelling reasons to join and become an active member of this organization for career-based reasons. However, throughout my professional life I have always found MLA invaluable not just for professional support but for the incredible moral support and collegiality it has provided me. I know from my conversations with others actively involved in larger, more formal professional organizations that this type of enveloping friendliness isn't necessarily true in other groups, no matter how worthy the organization may be. But it is a cornerstone of the Music Library Association experience for most members. I personally have found it to be so and I trust that others will agree with my assessment. MLA is more than a professional organization, it is a group of committed, caring individuals who are in turn wonderful mentors, colleagues, and ultimately, lifelong friends.

Notes

1. The best history of the Music Library Association from the beginning through the early 1980s is Carol June Bradley's *American Music Librarianship: A Biographical and Historical Survey* (New York: Greenwood, 1990). See chapter 7 for a detailed description of the founding and early years of MLA and its premier publication, *Notes*. As the book's title indicates, it is also an important reference tool for biographical details about the founding members of the profession as a whole.

2. Music Library Association website, www.musiclibraryassoc.org (20 April 2003). The home page serves as a gateway to the Association's numerous web pages, mentioned throughout the chapter.

3. MLA website.

4. Available, as are several other MLA series, from Scarecrow Press. See the Publications section on MLA's website, or www.scarecrowpress.com for more information (20 April 2003).

10

The International Association of Music Libraries

John Wagstaff

The International Association of Music Libraries, Archives and Documentation Centres, usually shortened to "IAML" (rhyming with "camel") was officially founded in Paris in 1951, although its roots go back to a meeting of music librarians held in Florence, Italy, in October 1949 in celebration of the 100th anniversary of the foundation of the Accademia Luigi Cherubini in that city. Exactly why the directors of the Florence conservatory decided to celebrate their anniversary in this way does not appear to have been recorded, but those who met in Paris two years afterward certainly felt that the Florence gathering had been of sufficient significance to justify its being regarded as the first meeting of the new Association, and for a further meeting in Lüneburg, Germany, in 1950 to be designated its second. As a result, the Paris congress, regarded by some as the first official meeting of the new body, was in fact designated IAML's third, not its first.

No organization, including IAML and MLA, springs forth fully formed, and the planning for what became IAML probably began soon after the conclusion in Europe of World War II in 1945. Certainly by late 1947 the United Nations Educational, Scientific and Cultural Organization (UNESCO) had resolved to set up an International Music Institute whose brief would include encouraging the foundation of new international organizations in fields of music where none currently existed, and an international association of music libraries would certainly have fallen into this category. An intriguing feature that perhaps distinguishes IAML from MLA, eighteen years its senior, during its early years and subsequently is the close connection between library and musicological agendas that have been a feature of IAML's meetings. The chair of the 1949 Florence congress, which included musicologists as well as librarians, was Friedrich Blume, first editor of the German-language music encyclopedia *Die Musik in Geschichte und Gegenwart* and president of the International Musicological Society at the time. IAML's Lüneburg meeting in 1950 was timed and located to coincide with a conference of the Gesellschaft für Musikforschung, and the agenda set for the new organization at that meeting strongly reflected a musicological outlook. A connection between IAML and UNESCO was another feature of the early years, and it is possible that IAML's organizational structure even today, with its council, board and triennial general assembly, and its work carried out by a mixture of professional branches, subject commissions, working groups, and committees, continues to owe something to this relationship. As usual in such situations, however, it is the people who make up the organization's membership who make it what it is and who breathe warmth into what can at first sight appear a rather forbidding institutional framework.

Just as MLA has a number of regional "chapters," IAML has a network of national branches that make up the whole. These national branches are an essential part of the organization and have always been encouraged by the parent body, since it is often through involvement with their national branch that IAML members become interested in participating at the international level. Both IAML and its national branches have grown significantly since its foundation, from 230 members in twenty countries in 1952 to 1,925 members in 60 countries in 2001. Some national branches are large—that of the United States remains numerically the biggest, with 271 members in 2001, followed by Germany (233 members in 2001), Italy and Spain (155 members each), the United Kingdom, and Sweden—while others, such as the New Zealand and Polish branches, are much smaller (respectively comprising 22 and 12 members in 2001), although it should be acknowledged straight away that many of these smaller branches punch well above their weight. Some national groups, such as the UK, Swiss, and German branches, were founded in the first few years after the 1951 Paris congress, while others are of much more recent date. A feature common to many national branches—though not to the U.S. branch, a fact that, in view of its size, is somewhat ironic—is the production of a regular newsletter or journal, some of which are quite substantial. The Canadian Association of Music Libraries, which serves as IAML's Canadian arm, issues a bilingual *CAML Review* several times a year; the Germans publish an important quarterly periodical, *Forum Musikbibliothek*, that sets a high standard for others to follow; and the recently established UK and Ireland branch (formerly the UK branch) has a twice-yearly newsletter, as well as its branch journal, *Brio*. Newsletters from New Zealand and Australia (which also publishes the annual journal *Continuo*), from several Scandinavian countries, and from the Netherlands and France keep members of those countries in touch with each other and typically provide a forum for news, research, and reports. Several national branches nowadays have their own electronic mailing lists and websites, and some organize at least an annual meeting, which allows members to get together: The United States is again slightly different from other branches in this regard, in that its IAML assembly usually takes place within the framework of an MLA annual meeting. Furthermore, the national branches occasionally make representations on members' behalf when music library services and music librarians' posts are under threat.

At the international level, IAML has its own website (currently at www.cilea.it/music/iaml/iamlhome.htm), its own electronic mailing list (iaml-l@cornell.edu), which all members can join, and—since 1999—its own electronic newsletter (at www.cilea.it/music/iaml/news/newsletter.htm). Among other things, the website includes contact details for those wishing to join the organization. IAML holds an annual meeting (variously called "conference" or "congress" depending on the presence or absence of a meeting of its general assembly), whose location changes each year. While the majority of the meetings since its foundation have taken place in Europe, it has several times met in the United States (including at Berkeley, California, in 2002), and in 1999 mounted its first conference in the southern hemisphere, at Wellington, New Zealand. A further southern trip is planned in 2007, when the meeting will be in Sydney, Australia. These meetings provide opportunities for members to make new contacts or to nurture old ones, as well as to hear reports on what is happening in music libraries around the globe. A regular feature is a session or two focusing on music and music librarianship in the host country, often in conjunction with a special issue of IAML's quarterly international journal, *Fontes Artis Musicae*. *Fontes* (as it is usually abbreviated) also carries reviews, reports, and essays on library, bibliographic, and musicological topics. For those members unable to attend the international meetings it is often the most direct and visible contact they have with "international" IAML (or, rather, that international IAML has with them). Consequently the journal also carries information on such matters as the Association's financial accounts, reports of its general meetings, information from its working groups, commissions, and committees, and news from the four "R" projects that it supports in collaboration with the International Musicological Society and other international bodies. Taken chronologically in order of foundation these are the *Répertoire International des Sources Musicales* (RISM); the *Répertoire International de Littérature Musicale* (RILM), an international inventory of music literature with which many music librarians will already have come into contact, either in print form or electronically via OCLC or another provider; the *Répertoire International d'Iconographie Musicale* (RidIM); and the RIPM, originally titled *Répertoire International de la Presse Musicale* but recently renamed the *Retrospective Index to Music Periodicals 1800–1950.* By its involvement in these and other projects, such as the "Documenta Musicologica" series of music facsimile publications, IAML continues to demonstrate its interest in a musicological agenda as well as in a purely "library-based" one. In a music library world often characterized by small teams of library staff working in comparatively small libraries, IAML offers its members a window on a national and international musical and music-library stage, together with a number of benefits ranging from publications and meetings to practical support in the workplace.

11

Coda

The Power of Music, or, Why Do Music Librarians Stay in the Profession?

Susan T. Sommer

I have to start this talk with a confession.[1] Unlike my colleagues who have spoken previously, I don't have any facts to give you. I haven't counted anything. I don't have any audiovisual aids. I didn't even write anything down. I was asked to respond to presentations on the topic "Why do people stay in the profession?," and I hoped I could come up with some impromptu remarks that would suffice. As it happens, the question has already been answered this morning. It is quite simple: people stay in our profession because they want to be music librarians.

Obviously we are not in this for the money. We know that. This subject has come up depressingly often today. And as we have heard, the fabulous opportunities for job advancement are clearly not an enticement. But there is one area that has not been addressed, but which I think is very important for us to consider and be aware of—our self-image, or to put it more grandly, our status within the entire society. We all feel a little awkward about this one. Let's face it, if you meet three people at a party, a corporate lawyer, an investment banker, and a brain surgeon, and you say you are a music librarian, do you expect them all to say "Oh, wow!"? You know they won't, so perhaps we are all a little shy about saying, "I'm a music librarian." We aren't really as proud of being music librarians as we should be. So I want to speak today to the subject of why we should want to be proud to be music librarians. And to do that I would like to ask you to shift your perspective from yourself to something much larger.

A friend of mine recently said that he was expecially fond of the weather channel on television because it was so bizarre. Here were all these people who only thought about weather all day long. Weather, weather, weather, you see . . . and compared to everything else on television perhaps it is bizarre. But that is compared to everything else on television—an odd universe to judge anything by. I started thinking about this, and it occurred to me—suppose you look at this from another perspective. Suppose you are an astronaut looking at this fragile little planet from way up in the cosmic sky. You look down, and what do you see? Weather! That's it. That's all there is . . . weather.

Weather had essentially created this planet. So, looked at from another direction, weather is it. Now, we're not going to be astronauts, but probably a lot of us are going to take a plane home tomorrow. And— weather permitting—as we look out of that plane, we will see our country and our world from another perspective. We will see mountains and hills and lakes, and some of the products of human endeavor, but we probably won't see any people because they're a little too small to be seen from that distance. Now, suppose you are looking at this view and describing it to a neighbor from outer space. There are these tiny things called people; You can't see them from up here but they are there, you say, and they have done all this work over many, many years, and they have created this society; they have worked together, and they have built all these things, and they each perform various functions. And some of these people have the task of maintaining the written record of everything this society has created. We call them librarians. "They must be very important," remarks your companion. I agree: Being a librarian *is* very important from this enormously long perspective.

Then, how about the personal perspective? We've heard quite a lot about that today. A number of people have responded to my colleagues, who have duly counted them, saying that they find librarianship intellectually involving, that they find satisfaction in creating and maintaining a systematic ordering of things. We have here, among other things, the wonder of technical services so eloquently described by Richard Smiraglia.[2]

Another aspect of librarianship that I think we find particularly meaningful is that compared to work in many sectors of our economy, it doesn't hurt anybody. Perhaps that's why we're not corporate lawyers or investment bankers or even brain surgeons.

Finally, librarianship is a cooperative calling, and it's fun to be cooperative. It's nice to be in a profession that asks you to cooperate with the public that uses your collection, whether they be students and professors, the general public, or a special clientele. You work with other librarians who are similarly inclined. You work with people who share similar values, and this carries an enormous personal reward. So a librarian is indeed a good thing to be.

Now, how about the other part of music librarianship? *Music.* Well, we all know that music matters. That it is really important. That it is basic to our being. How do you answer people who say that music is just a frill? Admittedly, sometimes music is a frill. I think that music in an elevator is a frill (and an ugly one). I think that a number of invasive uses of music in our society treat it as a frill. But precisely because of this we lose track of the fact that music is really essential to our lives. It isn't just that it's nice; it isn't just that it's pleasant. It is actually basic to not just the human, but the entire, experience of the world. I'd like to make a few little suggestions about how this can be.

Music, as we know, has enormous spiritual power. For example, music can carry joy around the world. Sam Orlinick, a wonderful antiquarian music dealer, once said that when Mozart died he left the world with more joy in it than had existed before he had been born. Think about that. I think it's a beautiful thought and I think it's probably true. Music and Mozart have extraordinary powers.

Remember that brain surgeon? Doctors don't always work on situations that are healable. But music, amazingly, can sometimes do more than any medicine. You know that. Those of you who have had a serious illness know that music can actually help heal the body, but even more than that—and this is really miraculous—music can help heal a broken heart. I'm sure some of you at least have found that out as well.

There are other ways music can affect us that are more unusual. For example, music can give us a different way of perceiving reality—literally through our brains. If you haven't read *The Man Who Mistook His Wife for a Hat* by Oliver Sacks, I insist that you go right out and buy it in paperback.[3] It is one of the most fascinating sets of essays that you will ever encounter by a very eminent neurologist who deals with problems that are physically located inside the brain. He describes people who are impaired in various ways of perception and their reaction to the world around them. The title story is about a music teacher who has lost the ability to perceive the kind of natural objects that would make his life a normal one. I won't go into details, but the interesting thing is that this man nevertheless succeeded—without realizing it—by substituting music for other patterns of logical connection within his brain. There are some other good music stories in the book that will reinforce the point. Look it up.

Another thought is that music contains among the most impressive achievements of mankind. Again I recommend a book to you. If you have not already read Lewis Thomas's *Lives of a Cell*, add that to your reading list.[4] There, a very distinguished scientist, again, looks at the humanities, at society, at the world as a whole. He has many meaningful things to say about music and at one point suggests that if we are going to try to reach out into space we can do better than simply beaming radio signals out there. Who cares if you go beep, beep, beep? Who would bother to answer? Instead, says Thomas, send the works of Johann Sebastian Bach. That would be something worth investigating! Because, of course, Bach's works are among the most important works that human beings have created. As you all know.

Finally, how about a really big, all-encompassing theory? Boethius, the great fourth-century encyclopedist, expressed the belief of centuries of medieval philosophers that what we hear as music is actually the aural representation of the natural order and proportion that governs the universe. Think on that. Wow! And don't discount these men because they lived a long time ago. Most of them were a lot smarter than you are; they just looked at things from a different perspective.

So those are a couple of reasons for staying in the profession. Because of librarianship. Because of music. And on a lighter—but no less important—note, because you can go to MLA meetings! Looking out at all of you, I see a great number of people who are lovely, wonderful, nice folks. All of you do not know each other yet, but I hope that you will know more of each other by the time this and other meetings are over, and that you will be able to work cooperatively for many years in this wonderful profession that we share.

Notes

1. This address was delivered in 1988 at the annual meeting of the Music Library Association, and was subsequently published as a transcription in *Careers in Music Librarianship: Perspectives from the Field*, comp. Carol Tatian, MLA Technical Report, 18. (Canton, MA: The Music Library Association, 1990): 77–81. The text of that publication appears here, with modest revisions by the author, for inclusion in the present volume. Reprinted with permission of the Music Library Association.—Ed.

2. This refers to a talk presented in the same session by Richard P. Smiraglia, "Careers in Music Technical Services," the text of which was also published in *Careers* (1990): 67–76.—Ed.

3. Oliver Sacks, *The Man Who Mistook his Wife for a Hat* (New York: Summit Books, 1985).

4. Lewis Thomas, *The Lives of a Cell: Notes of a Biology Watcher* (New York: Viking Press, 1974).

Selected Resources

Laurel A. Whisler

This selection of books, articles, and web pages provides an overview of the music library profession. The entries include works on music librarianship in general, types of music librarians, the education of music librarians, and the work performed by music librarians. The resource list was compiled largely from searches of the following databases: Dissertation Abstracts, Arts and Humanities Citation Index, Library Literature, Music Index, International Index to Music Periodicals, and OCLC's WorldCat.

For the sake of currency and usefulness to the Music Library Association audience, resources published since 1990 (the publication date of the first edition of this work) from a general (i.e., nonnational) or specifically North American perspective have been included. Some exceptions are publications on copyright that include issues pertaining to the European Union and the exclusion of articles on technology where the software or applications described were largely outdated by 2003. Articles about the history of specific collections or libraries have also been excluded.

General

Much has been published on the history and role of music librarians. Guides to our work and other practical tools are included as well.

Adamson, Danette Cook, and Mimi Tashiro. "Servants, Scholars, and Sleuths: Early Leaders in California Music Librarianship." *Notes* 48, no. 3 (March 1992): 806–35.

Bradley, Carol June. *American Music Librarianship: A Biographical and Historical Survey.* New York: Greenwood, 1990.

Davidson, Mary Wallace. "American Music Libraries and Librarianship: Challenges for the Nineties." *Notes* 50, no. 1 (1993): 13–22.

French, Richard F. "Remarks at a Symposium on Music Librarianship in America, Harvard University, October 7, 1989." *Notes* 46, no. 3 (March 1990): 846–48.

Griscom, Richard, and Amanda Maple. *Music Librarianship at the Turn of the Century.* Music Library Association Technical Reports 27. Lanham, MD: Scarecrow, 2000.

Hayes, Helen. "Sounding Brass or Tinkling Triangle: The Role of Librarians and Information Professionals to the Year 2000." *Continuo* 25 (1996): 1–3.

International Association of Music Libraries, Archives and Documentation Centres. www.cilea.it/music/iaml/iamlhome.htm (20 May 2003).

Koehler, William Alan. "A Music Professor Views Music Libraries." *Music Reference Services Quarterly* 1, no. 2 (1992): 41–49.

Ledsham, Ian. *Music Librarianship: The Comprehensive Guide to Music Librarianship.* Aberystwyth: Open Learning Unit Deptartment of Information and Library Studies, University of Wales, 2000.

Lesniaski, David. "A Profile of the Music Library Association Membership." *Notes* 56, no. 4 (June 2000): 894–906.

McKeon, Edward. "On the Shelf." *Music Scholar* (Spring 1997): 23, 25.

Music Library Association. www.musiclibraryassoc.org. (20 May 2003). Placement Service. "Placement Service Job List." www.musiclibraryassoc.org/services/se_job.htm (20 May 2003).

Ochs, Michael, and Richard F. French. *Music Librarianship in America: Papers of a Symposium Held 5-7 October 1989 Honoring the Establishment of the Richard F. French Librarianship at Harvard*

Univerity. Cambridge: Eda Kuhn Loeb Music Library, Harvard University, 1991.

Pope, Janice. "A Selected Annotated Bibliography of the Literature of Music Librarianship, 1973–1982." Master's thesis, University of North Carolina at Chapel Hill, 1992.

Roberts, Don. "The Byte Makes the Bachs More Accessible: Dynamic Changes in Music Librarianship." *Continuo* 25 (1996): 4–7.

Schnackenberg, Karen. "Technology and Tradition." *International Musician* 96 (July 1997): 11.

Smith, Carleton Sprague, Israel J. Katz, et al. *Libraries, History, Diplomacy, and the Performing Arts: Essays in Honor of Carleton Sprague Smith*. Stuyvesant, NY: Pendragon, 1991.

Studwell, William Emmett. "Where Is the Mainstream of Music in the Late Twentieth Century? A Heretical Look at Shifts in American Culture and Their Implications for Music Libraries." *Music Reference Services Quarterly* 4, no. 1 (1995): 43–48.

Tatian, Carol, comp. *Careers in Music Librarianship: Perspectives from the Field*. MLA Technical Report, 18. Canton, MA: Music Library Association, 1990.

Turbet, Richard. "Endangered Species." *The Musical Times* 133 (August 1992): 396.

———. "Hidden Resources: Music Librarians in Conference." *The Musical Times* 132 (August 1991): 389–90.

Wagstaff, John. "Some Recent Articles on Music Librarianship." *Brio* 37 (Spring/Summer 2000): 22–23.

———. "Some Recent Articles on Music Librarianship." *Brio* 37 (Autumn/Winter 2000): 48–49.

Walker, Diane Parr. "Music in the Academic Library of Tomorrow." *Notes* 59, no. 4 (June 2003): 817–27.

Education for Music Librarianship

Included in this section are articles about the initial education and professional development of librarians and training of staff, a list of core competencies, and library schools with course offerings in music librarianship.

Carobine, Timothy. "Education and Training for Music Catalogers in the United States." *Fontes Artis Musicae* 38, no. 1 (1991): 61–67.

Cherubini, Timothy J., comp. and ed. "Directory of Library School Offerings in Music Librarianship." 7th ed. Education Committee, Music Library Association, 1998. www.musiclibraryassoc/services/se_schoo.htm. (20 May 2003).

Duggan, Mary Kay. "Teaching Music Librarians Through Very Large Databases: Local Online Catalogs, OCLC, and RLIN." *Fontes Artis Musicae* 40, no. 3 (July/September 1993): 191–97.

Hart, Liz, and Ruth Hellen. "Music for the Terrified: Basic Music Courses for Library Staff." *Fontes Artis Musicae* 47, no. 1 (January/March 2000): 22–26.

Marley, Judith L. "Education for Music Librarianship Within the United States: Content Analysis of Selected Documentation and Structured Interviews with Selected Practitioners." Ph.D. diss., University of Pittsburgh, 2000.

———. "Education for Music Librarianship Within the United States: Needs and Opinions of Recent Graduate/Practitioners." *Fontes Artis Musicae* 49, no. 3 (July/September 2002): 139–72.

McConnell, Kristen. "The Professional Development of Music Librarians." Master's thesis, University of North Carolina at Chapel Hill, 2002.

Morrow, Jean. "Education for Music Librarianship." *Notes* 56, no. 3 (March 2000): 655–61.

Music Library Association. Library School Liaison Subcommittee. "Core Competencies and Music Librarians." www.musiclibraryassoc.org/pdf/Core_Competencies.pdf (20 May 2003).

Types of Music Librarians

Implicit in the following section on the work of music librarians is the librarian's placement within an academic or public library context. Certainly other types of music librarians exist, notably the orchestra librarian.

"Behind the Scenes: A Roundtable (Librarians of Symphony Orchestras Exchange Ideas)." *Harmony* 9 (October 1999): 61–71.

Blackley, Christi Birch. "An Overview of Orchestra Librarianship." Master's thesis, University of North Carolina at Chapel Hill, 1995.

Faulkner, H. "Broadcasting and Orchestra Libraries." *Fontes Artis Musicae* 39, no. 1 (January/March 1992): 23.

Holmes, Andrew S. "Classification of the Performance Librarian Within the Orchestra." Bachelor's thesis, Drew University, 1998.

Major Orchestra Librarians' Association. Publication Committee. "The Orchestra Librarian: A Career Introduction." 1993, rev. 2001. www.mola–inc.org/orchlib.html (20 May 2003)

"Many Hats Behind the Music: For Librarians It's a Constant Work in Progress." *International Musician* 100, no. 8 (August 2002): 13.

Music Library Association. "Music Librarianship—Is It For You?" www.musiclibraryassoc.org/isit/isit.htm (20 may 2003).

Ruhe, Pierre. "Crisis Manager." *The Strad* 108, no. 1285 (May 1997): 584.

Schnackenberg, Karen. "The Orchestra Librarian." *International Musician* 91 (July 1992): 18.

———."Orchestra Librarians Keep Up in Digital Age." *International Musician* 100 (July 2002): 9.

Shoaf, R. Wayne. "Archives." *Notes* 56, no. 3 (March 2000): 648–654.

Stevens, Clare. "Just the Job: Company Music Librarian." *Classical Music* 604 (11 April 1998): 38.

———. "Just the Job: Music Hire Librarian." *Classical Music* 636 (10 July 1999): 31.

Tice, Beth Elene. "Two Hats, One Heart: Confessions of a Split Position Librarian at the University of Minnesota Music Library." *Technicalities* 18, no. 7 (July/August 1998): 4–6.

The Work of Music Librarians

This section offers a glimpse of the complexity and variety of work in which music librarians are engaged and provides an interesting and useful literature survey for current practitioners.

Cataloging, Classification, Metadata, and Authority Work

Cassaro, James P. "Music Cataloguing and the Future." *Fontes Artis Musicae* 41, no. 3 (1994): 245–50.

Coover, James B. "Musical Ephemera: Some Thoughts About Types, Controls, Access." In *Foundations in Music Bibliography*. New York: Haworth Press, 1993.

Coral, Lenore, et al. "Automation Requirements for Music Information." *Notes* 43, no. 1 (1986): 1–18.

"The Core Bibliographic Record for Music and Sound Recordings." *Fontes Artis Musicae* 45, no. 2 (April/June 1998): 139–51.

Elliker, Calvin Harold. "Classification Schemes for Scores: Analysis of Structural Levels." *Notes* 50, no. 4 (1994): 1269–1320.

Eriksen, Dawn A., and William Emmett Studwell. "Music Libraries and a Subject Heading Code." *Music Reference Services Quarterly* 1, no. 1 (1992): 73–75.

Fling, R. Michael. "Automated Formatting of Music Bibliographic Records." *Music Reference Services Quarterly* 1, no. 3 (1993): 83–94.

Hemmasi, Harriette. "The Music Thesaurus: Function and Foundations." *Notes* 50, no. 3 (March 1994): 875–82.

Hogg, Katharine. "Music Libraries Online—A Virtual Union Catalogue for Music." *Fontes Artis Musicae* 47, no. 1 (January/March 2000): 14–21.

Jung, Karen. "Online Systems and the Music Backlog: Highway to Efficiency, or Roadway to Ruin?" *Music Reference Services Quarterly* 3, no. 1 (1994): 63–75.

MacLeod, Judy. "When Reclassification and Retrospective Conversion Interrupt Reference." *Music Reference Services Quarterly* 4, no. 2 (1995): 11–19.

MacLeod, Judy, and Kim Lloyd. "A Study of Music Cataloging Backlogs." *Library Resources and Technical Services* 38 (January 1994): 7–15.

McKee, E. A. "Cataloging System Review." *ARSC Journal* 27, no. 1 (1996): 59–64.

Papakhian, A. Ralph. "Cataloging." *Notes* 56, no. 3 (March 2000): 581–90.

Smiraglia, Richard P. "Beyond the Score." *Notes* 54, no. 3 (March 1998): 649–66.

———. "Musical Works and Information Retrieval." *Notes* 58, no. 4 (June 2002): 747–64.

Studwell, William Emmett. "Music Libraries and the Possible Collapse of the Cataloging Process." *Music Reference Services Quarterly* 1, no. 3 (1993): 79–81.

Vellucci, Sherry Lynn. "Bibliographic Relationships and the Future of Music Catalogues." *Fontes Artis Musicae* 45, nos. 3–4 (July/December 1998): 213–26.

————. "Metadata for Music—Issues and Directions (Dublin Core Element Set)." *Fontes Artis Musicae* 46, nos. 3–4 (July/December 1999): 205–17.

————. "Music Metadata and Authority Control in an International Context." *Notes* 57, no. 3 (March 2001): 541–54.

Yee, Martha M. "Musical Works on OCLC; or, What if OCLC Were Actually to Become a Catalog?" *Music Reference Services Quarterly* 8, no. 1 (2001): 1–26.

Collection Management

Gottlieb, Jane. "Collection Assessment in Music Libraries." *Fontes Artis Musicae* 45, no. 2 (April/June 1998): 193–94.

Hack, Rosalinda I., and Richard C. Schwegel. "Music Collections." In *Managing Performing Arts Collections in Academic and Public Libraries*. Westport, CT: Greenwood, 1994.

Kuyper–Rushing, Lois. "Music Libraries: Centralization Versus Decentralization." *College and Research Libraries* 63, no. 2 (March 2002): 139–49.

Maple, Amanda, and Jean Morrow. *Guide to Writing Collection Development Policies for Music*. Lanham, MD: Scarecrow, 2001.

Music Library Association. New England Chapter. "Music Collection and Acquisition Practices in Connecticut Public Libraries." *Public Libraries* 39, no. 6 (November/December 2000): 348–55.

Zager, Daniel. "Collection Development and Management." *Notes* 56, no. 3 (March 2000): 567–73.

Copyright

Barrows, Lorraine. "Managing Your Music Library." *The Pitch Pipe* 54, no. 4 (April 2002): 14–15.

Davidson, Mary Wallace. "Copyright." *Notes* 56, no. 3 (March 2000): 598–604.

Music Library Association. "Copyright for Music Librarians." www.lib.jmu.edu/org/mla (Accessed May 20, 2003).

Pope, Alan. "Harmonization of EC Copyright Protection: A Music
    Libraries View." *Brio* 32, no. 1 (1995): 20–23.

Information Systems and Digitization

Abbott, Gordon, and Mary O'Mara. "Audio on the Web: Applications in
    Academic Music Libraries." *Continuo* 28 (1999): 1–11.
Davidson, Mary Wallace. "Trends and Issues in Digital Technology."
    Fontes Artis Musicae 48, no. 4 (October/December 2001): 398–
    410.
Dunn, John, and Constance A. Mayer. "VARIATIONS: A Digital Music
    Library System at Indiana University." In *DL '99: Proceedings of
    the Fourth ACM Conference on Digital Libraries*, Berkeley,
    California, 12–19 August 1999. Reprinted at www.dlib.indiana.edu/
    variations/VARIATIONS–DL99.pdf (20 May 2003).
Fineman, Yale. "The Economics of Information: DW3 and the Case for
    Creating a Music Megasite." *Notes* 58, no. 3 (March 2002): 504–
    10.
Greenwald, Ted. "On line Services Poised to Take Over Everything."
    Musician 195 (January/February 1995): 50.
Griscom, Richard. "Distant Music: Delivering Audio Over the Internet."
    Notes 59, no. 3 (March 2003): 521–41.
Maple, Amanda, and Tona A. Henderson. "Prelude to a Digital Music
    Library at the Pennsylvania State University: Networking Audio for
    Academic Library Users." *Library Resources and Technical Services*
    44, no. 4 (October 2000): 190–95.
"Variations2: Indiana University Digital Music Library Project." http://
    variations2.indiana.edu/. (20 May 2003).
Wright, H. Stephen. "Technology." *Notes* 56, no. 3 (March 2000): 591–
    97.

Preservation

Blaine, Susan, and Janet Gertz. "Preservation of Printed Music: The
    Columbia University Libraries Scores Condition Survey." *Fontes
    Artis Musicae* 41, no. 3 (July/September 1994): 261–69.
Carli, Alice. *Binding and Care of Printed Music*. Music Library
    Association Basic Manual Series 2. Lanham, MD: Scarecrow, 2003.

"Disaster Preparedness: Tales from the Front." *CAML Newsletter* 27 (April 1999): 11–12.

Honea, Sion M. "Preservation at the Sibley Music Library of the Eastman School of Music." *Notes* 53, no. 2 (1996): 381–402.

Nelson–Strauss, Brenda. "Preservation Policies and Priorities for Recorded Sound Collections." *Notes* 48, no. 2 (1991): 425–36.

Shepard, John. "Preservation." *Notes* 56, no. 3 (March 2000): 57–80.

Sommer, Susan Thiemann. "Knowing the Score: Preserving Collections of Music." *Fontes Artis Musicae* 41, no. 3 (July/September 1994): 256–60.

Warren, Richard. "Storage of Sound Recordings." *ARSC Journal* 24, no. 2 (1993): 130–75.

Reference

Caleb, Peter. "Opera on the Internet: Library Resources on the Internet." *The Opera Quarterly* 16 (Autumn 2000): 633–38.

Casey, Jeanette, and Kathryn Taylor. "Music Library Users: Who Are These People and What Do They Want From Us?" *Music Reference Services Quarterly* 3, no. 3 (1995): 3–14.

Christensen, Beth Elaine, Mary J. Du Mont, and Alan Green. "Taking Note: Assessing the Performance of Reference Service in Academic Music Libraries: A Progress Report." *Notes* 58, no. 1 (September 2001): 39–54.

Churchwell, Cynthia. "Internet Accessible Resources Containing Information About Sound Recordings." *ARSC Journal* 27, no. 2 (1996): 171–87.

Gottlieb, Jane. "Reference Service for Performing Musicians: Understanding and Meeting Their Needs." *The Reference Librarian* 47 (1994): 47–59.

Hunter, David. "Two Half-Centuries of Music Bibliography." *Notes* 50, no. 1 (September 1993): 23–38.

Lasocki, David. "Music Reference as a Calling: An Essay." *Notes* 56, no. 4 (June 2000): 879–93.

———. "Reference." *Notes* 56, no. 3 (March 2000): 605–10.

MacLeod, Judy. "When Reclassification and Retrospective Conversion Interrupt Reference." *Music Reference Services Quarterly* 4, no. 2 (1995): 11–19.

Poroila, Heikki. "Children and the Music Library." *Fontes Artis Musicae* 48, no. 3 (July/September 2001): 246–49.

Studwell, William E. "Tracking Down Elusive Songs: Four Examples of Problem Solving in Music Libraries." *Music Reference Services Quarterly* 4, no. 1 (1995): 69–75.

User Education

Christensen, Beth E. "Building on Tonic: Integrating Information Literacy Into the Music Curriculum." *College Music Symposium* 41 (2001): 1–6.

———. "Music Library Association Projects on Bibliographic Instruction." *Music Reference Services Quarterly* 2, nos. 1–2 (1993): 153–56.

Christensen, Beth Elaine, and Gerald Hoekstra. "Being Here, Being There: Understanding Early Music Through Historical Research and Analysis." *Research Strategies* 9 (Spring 1991): 106–10.

Clark, Caryl Leslie, and Suzanne Meyers Sawa. "Faculty–Librarian Cooperation in Bibliographic Instruction." *CAML Newsletter* 26 (April 1998): 17–20.

Farber, Evan. "General Principles of Bibliographic Instruction." In *Foundations in Music Bibliography*. New York: Haworth Press, 1993.

Fenske, David Edward. "A Core Literature for Music Bibliography In *Foundations in Music Bibliography*. New York: Haworth Press, 1993.

Fidler, Linda M., and Richard S. James. "Integrating Library User Education with the Undergraduate Music History Sequence." In *Foundations in Music Bibliography*. New York: Haworth Press, 1993.

Fling, R. Michael. "Music Bibliographic Instruction on Microcomputers: Part I." In *Foundations in Music Bibliography*. New York: Haworth Press, 1993. Originally published in *Music Reference Services Quarterly* 2, nos. 1/2.

Germer, Mark. "Whither Bibliographic Instruction for Musicians?" *Notes* 52, no. 3 (March 1996): 754–60.

Hall, Alison, and Gail J. Sonnemann. "Establishing an Instructional Program for Music Users of Online Catalogs: Concepts, Options and Priorities." *Fontes Artis Musicae* 37, no. 2 (April/June 1990): 138–49.

Maple, Amanda, Beth Elaine Christensen, and Kathleen A. Abromeit. "Information Literacy for Undergraduate Music Students: A Conceptual Framework." *Notes* 52 (March 1996): 744–53.

Marley, Judith L., "Bibliographic and User Instruction Within Music Libraries: An Overview of Teaching Methodologies." *Music Reference Services Quarterly* 6, no. 3 (1998): 33–44.

Marley, Judith L., and Harry E. Price. "Bringing Music History Alive: Using Artifacts to Explore Historiography." *Research Strategies* 10 (Summer 1992): 134–37.

Royse, Molly P., and Rosita M. Sands. "Bibliographic Instruction and Afro–American Music: An Experience in Faculty–Librarian Cooperation." *Research Strategies* 8 (Winter 1990): 40–43.

Talalay, Kathryn Marguerite. "Music Bibliographic Instruction on Microcomputers: Part II." In *Foundations in Music Bibliography*. New York: Haworth Press, 1993.

Troutman, Leslie. "User Education in Music Libraries." *Notes* 56, no. 3 (March 2000): 620–27.

Watanabe, Ruth Taiko. "Teaching Bibliography to Performers in a University School of Music." In *Foundations in Music Bibliography*. New York: Haworth Press, 1993.

Index

About the Contributors

LINDA W. BLAIR is cataloging coordinator at the Sibley Music Library, Eastman School of Music, where she has been a member of the cataloging staff since 1989. She also works occasionally at the Sibley reference desk and provides bibliographic instruction for Eastman's Music Education graduate students, as well as serving as a general liaison to the Music Education Department. Formerly chair of the MLA Personnel Subcommittee, she currently serves on the Education Committee. She has served as chair of the New York State/Ontario Chapter of MLA (twice), newsletter editor, and chair of the Travel Grants Committee. Other professional memberships include MOUG (the Music OCLC Users Group), the Rochester Flute Association, and the Rochester Alumnae Chapter of Sigma Alpha Iota, where she serves as financial advisor to the Eastman student chapter. She has earned degrees from Lebanon Valley College (B.S., music education, flute), Cornell University (M.S., adult, continuing and extension education/educational psychology), and Southern Connecticut State University (M.L.S.).

Like many people, Linda arrived at music librarianship via a circuitous route. After four years of teaching in public schools, she entered Cornell University's program in adult, continuing and extension Education, where she pursued research interests centered on lifelong learning in music. She married while living in Ithaca, and after completing her master's degree, moved with her husband to New Haven, Connecticut, so that he could attend medical school. Since she had loved the magnificent library system at Cornell, she looked for work in the Yale Library system and found a part-time job doing retrospective conversion at the Music Library. While she was there, Harold Samuel encouraged her to consider enrolling in library school, which she attended while working full-time. Immediately after graduation (seven months after the birth of twin daughters), her family relocated to Rochester, New York, where she found a part-time position in retrospective conversion at the Sibley Library, Eastman School of Music, which led to a position as catalog librarian, and eventually to her present position, which she has held since 1998.

JEANETTE L. CASEY has worked as music bibliographer, music recordings librarian, catalog librarian, first assistant, public services librarian, and "acting head," a phrase that was a source of amusement to her family. The libraries where she has worked are similarly varied: Chicago Public Library, California Western School of Law, Monash University (Australia), and Northwestern University. An active member of MLA for over twenty years, she has given numerous presentations at annual conferences and has served on the Information Sharing Subcommittee and as chair of the Public Libraries Committee and the Personnel Subcommittee. About her choice of music librarianship as a career, she notes: "It was obvious early on that there was no way I was going to make a living as a performer. I enjoyed working in libraries as an undergraduate and both of my grandmothers had been happy as librarians. Going into music librarianship seemed the perfect solution. So, I went straight into library school after getting my bachelor's degree. It took me a year to be hired as a music librarian, but it was worth the wait. I'm surrounded by music and help people who enjoy it, perform it, or are learning about it."

LAURA DANKNER, president of the Music Library Association, is associate professor emeritus at Loyola University in New Orleans. She served as head of the Loyola Music Library and an adjunct instructor in Loyola's College of Music from 1979 to 2002. Currently she is a part-time instructor in music appreciation at a state university. She received her bachelor's degree in voice from Ithaca College, her M.L.S. from the State University of New York at Albany, and a graduate degree in music education and voice from Brooklyn College, where she was also an adjunct instructor. Prior to assuming her position at Loyola, she was a professional singer in New York. She recalls several early influences on her decision to become a music librarian, saying, "I was fortunate to have met Walter Gerboth during those early years. Walter was a mentor to many music librarians and young teachers throughout his years as librarian and professor of music at Brooklyn College. Although at the time I thought my future path lay in teaching music at the college level, I think that subconsciously Walter had a great deal of influence on my decision, several years later, to become a music librarian. Like so many of my colleagues, I think that music librarianship found me! I had always loved libraries and came from a family of voracious readers. My earliest memories revolve around story hours at the main branch of the Brooklyn Public Library, a wonderful institution that also provided me with the opportunity to use a music library. Their collection of music scores stood me in good stead when I entered the High School of Music and Art (now La Guardia High School) in New York as a voice major."

Laura attended library school while living in a small town in western Massachusetts, commuting over the mountains to Albany. Her first job was as a "one-man-band" in a tiny private junior college library in Lenox, Massachusetts, where she did everything from administration to cataloging to reference. She regards this experience as very good training for her next job in the small academic music library that she spent twenty-two years running. She is the coauthor (with Grace Lichtenstein) of *Musical Gumbo* (Norton, 1993), and has been a reviewer of books and musical scores for *Notes*.

PAULA ELLIOT is currently architecture and performing arts librarian at Washington State University Libraries, where she has also been music reference librarian and head of humanities collection development. She earned the B.A. in music at Bard College, the M.L.S. at Syracuse, and subsequently acquired master's degrees in both music and theater while working full-time as a librarian. With a checkered background in interdisciplinary humanities and the responsibility for numerous subjects throughout her library career, Paula regards her longtime specialization in music as the mainstay of her professional life. She has served on the Music Library Association's Development Committee and Education Committee and was elected to a term as member-at-large of MLA's Board of Directors. For the organization's Personnel Subcommittee, she has hosted several workshops on employment-related issues, involvement that led to the present publication. Other professional affiliations include the American Musicological Society and Early Music America. She is the author of *Pro-Musica—Patronage, Performance and a Periodical: An Index to the Quarterlies, 1923–1929* (Music Library Association, 1992), articles, reviews, and encyclopedia entries.

Closer to home, Paula has been chair of the Pacific Northwest Chapter of MLA. She holds an adjunct faculty appointment in the Washington State University School of Music and Theatre Arts and has taught music bibliography to graduate students at WSU and the University of Idaho. As a performer, she sings professionally with a renaissance music ensemble, participates in a community chorus, and has been known to entertain with the occasional jazz standard.

RENÉE MCBRIDE has been humanities and music cataloger at the University of California, Los Angeles, since 1994. Prior to that she was fine arts cataloger at the University of Oklahoma, and she received her education at Baylor University (B.M., music theory) and the University of Iowa (M.A., music theory; M.A., library and information science). In addition to cataloging, Renée provides reference service in the UCLA Music Library a few hours per week. Her current professional activities include serving MLA as liaison to the International Alliance for Women in Music placement officer and board member-at-large. She also serves as an abstractor for *Reference Reviews Europe Online*. Recent publications include an article about harpist/composer Anne LeBaron in *Women and Music in America Since 1900: An Encyclopedia*, edited by Kristine H. Burns (Greenwood, 2002). Renée enjoys the opportunities afforded by music librarianship to bring together once seemingly disparate strands of learning and experience, and she appreciates that music librarianship often allows one to work in the humanities and other arts as well.

JEAN MORROW is director of libraries at the New England Conservatory in Boston, where she was formerly head of Technical Services. She earned her B.A. in humanities from MacMurray College, her M.A. in music history from Smith College, and is a doctoral candidate in musicology at New York University. She also holds an appointment as lecturer in the Simmons College Graduate School of Library and Information Science and has served as the president of the New England Chapter of MLA. Among her many publications are the *Guide to Writing Collection Development Policies for Music* (coauthor, Scarecrow, 2001), and the article "Education for Music Librarianship in the U.S. in the 21st Century," (*Fontes Artis Musicae*, 2002) which was first presented to the International Association of Music Libraries. She also contributed

"Education for Music Librarianship" to *Music Librarianship at the Turn of the Century* (Scarecrow, 2000). "As a graduate student in musicology for several years," Jean says, "I eagerly accepted my first library position as cataloging assistant where my work drew heavily on my knowledge of music history, primary sources and editions, and bibliographic tools. Throughout my library career, I have welcomed the opportunity to share my knowledge and love of music with the patrons who use my library."

NED QUIST got into music librarianship by a fortunate accident. As he was finishing his master's degree in music history at the Peabody Conservatory, the Peabody music librarian moved to another job. On the recommendation of a faculty member, Ned applied for a job at the Peabody library, thinking that someone already in the library would be promoted to head librarian, creating a vacancy that he could fill as an assistant. Much to his surprise, Ned was offered the position of head librarian—on a temporary basis. This temporary position lasted for twenty-five years, during which time he obtained his M.L.S. from Catholic University and enjoyed opportunities to participate in building a new library, become a part-time faculty member teaching music bibliography, and coordinate several IT projects on the Peabody campus.

He also became an active member of MLA, where he has served on the board as fiscal officer and as the convention manager. In 2001, he decided he wanted to return to his native New England and once again found good fortune in being named the music librarian at Brown University, where he is today. A folksinger and guitarist, Ned was a member of the trio Cross Country from 1988 to 1993 and now plays with a popular New England contradance band called White Squall.

SUSAN T. SOMMER's career at the New York Public Library began with a part-time job in the reading room of the landmark on 42nd Street building, "picking out shelf list cards for the RISM inventory." At her retirement in 2001, she was executive director of the New York Public Library for the Performing Arts at Lincoln Center, where she had earlier served as head of circulating collections and chief of the Music Division. She also taught in the library school at Columbia University, wrote reviews of early music for *High Fidelity*, and sang professionally. She has been the president of the Music Library Association and the editor of its journal, *Notes*. She continues to serve the music library world in many ways and is currently chair of the Greater New York Chapter of MLA.

She holds the B.A. degree from Smith College and the M.L.S. and D.Phil. from Columbia University.

During her "odd-job days," Suki says, she had the memorable experience of being a general assistant—what she calls "dog's body"—to Noah Greenberg, the founder of the historic ensemble, The New York Pro Musica. Reflecting on early professional influences, she remembers the significance of her first MLA meeting in Toronto in 1970 and notes the kindness and support that she experienced there as a newcomer to the profession. A generous mentor to younger music librarians, she has transmitted that same encouragement to succeeding generations.

SHERIDAN STORMES holds B.M. and M.M. degrees in vocal performance from Butler University and an M.S. in library science from Indiana University. She became interested in librarianship while working as an undergraduate student assistant in the Jordan College of Fine Arts Library at Butler. Sheri has been a librarian at Butler University for twenty-seven years. During that time she has served in various capacities, including associate music and fine arts librarian, associate director for Public Services, acting director of libraries, associate dean of libraries, and music and fine arts librarian. For several years, Sheri was chair of the Butler Libraries' Personnel Committee, and she has served on numerous search committees for various positions on the Butler campus.

Since 1988, Sheri has served as an adjunct instructor for the Jordan College of Fine Arts and has taught English, Italian, French, and German diction to singers, as well as an honors undergraduate course in music research techniques, and has team-taught the graduate music research course. Sheri has served on the Membership, Nominating, and Public Services Committees of MLA's Midwest Chapter, the Personnel Subcommittee of MLA, and the Continuing Education Committee of ALA's College Library Section. She is a member and past National Associate Regent of Pi Kappa Lambda. Sheri also is an active performer and vocal adjudicator in the Indianapolis area. She is a member of NATS and is alto soloist at First Baptist Church of Indianapolis. She is a member of Beta Phi Mu and Phi Kappa Phi.

GORDON THEIL is the head of the Music and Arts Libraries at UCLA, including their Special Collections Departments. He has an M.A. in music from UCLA and an M.L.S. from UC Berkeley. His publications include *Michael Tippett: A Bio-Bibliography* (Greenwood, 1989) and a modest number of articles and book reviews in various journals. He is a past member of the MLA Board of Directors, program chair of the MLA 1988 Annual Meeting in Minneapolis, past chair of MLA's Southern California Chapter, cofounder and coordinator of the Jewish Music Roundtable, and currently a member of the Association's Legislation Committee, among a number of other positions he has held in the Association over the last twenty years.

A one-time violist da gamba, having lost his instrument in the Los Angeles earthquake of 1993, he is currently blowing trombone and can be heard annually with the MLA Big Band.

JOHN WAGSTAFF has been music faculty librarian of Oxford University since 1988. Prior to that he worked in the music library of King's College, University of London. His decision to become a music librarian was the result of several factors. He wanted to do something practical with his musical degree qualifications, he wanted to do a job that involved helping others in some way, and he needed to support himself financially while undertaking his master's degree in musicology in London. He volunteered for general library work at his college, liked it, and stayed. His involvement with IAML goes back almost twenty years and has included a spell on the executive committee of IAML's United Kingdom branch. He has also been editor of the UK branch journal, *Brio*, the second edition of the *British Union Catalogue of Music Periodicals* (Ashgate, 1998), and since 2000, IAML's international journal, *Fontes Artis Musicae*.

John's musicological interests center on French music, particularly the music of Gabriel Faure. He contributed a bio-bibliography of Faure's great friend, the operetta and opera composer Andre Messager, to Greenwood Press's Bio-Bibliographies in Music series and several articles on minor French musicians of the 19th century to the second edition of *The New Grove*. His other publications include articles on Charles Burney and John Hawkins for the 2004 edition of the *British Dictionary of National Biography*, and work of early music publishers for the latest edition of the *Oxford Companion to Music*.

LAUREL A. WHISLER is music librarian at the Robert J. Maxwell Jr. Media Center at Furman University in Greenville, South Carolina, where she is also an adjunct instructor in the music department. Previously she was a reference librarian at Hanover College in Indiana. Laurel is an active member of the Music Library Association, where she serves on two committees, and she is member-at-large in the Southeast Chapter of the Music Library Association. She is also a member of the College Music Society and American Musicological Society. Her article, "Building a Better Reference Interface," appeared in *Internet Reference Services Quarterly* (1998).

Armed with a B.A. in music from Earlham College and an M.A. in music from The Pennsylvania State University, she began a Ph.D. in musicology at Indiana University, withdrawing to attend seminary for a year. After working for a used car dealership, an ice cream shop, and a bookstore, she took out more student loans, fell into a nearly full-time job at the Payton Philanthropic Studies Library at Indiana University-Purdue University, Indianapolis, and enrolled in evening classes for her M.L.S. Since she had a musical background, she completed the Specialization in Music Librarianship on the Bloomington campus. At Furman University she is the sole librarian in a branch library in the music building, where she oversees all aspects of the library.

H. STEPHEN WRIGHT is associate dean for Public Services in the Northern Illinois University Libraries in DeKalb; he was also music librarian at NIU for seventeen years. He is active in the Music Library Association and is currently editor of MLA's Technical Reports Series; he is also a former chair of the MLA Midwest Chapter and the Music OCLC Users Group. He has written extensively on the topic of music in films. His publications include *Keeping Score: Film and Television Music, 1980–1988* (Scarecrow, 1991), *Film Music Bibliography 1* (Society for the Preservation of Film Music, 1995), *Film Music Collections in the United States: A Guide* (Society for the Preservation of Film Music, 1996), and *Film Music at the Piano* (Scarecrow, 2003).